THE LEGEND

STEVE WARD WITH JOHN BRINDLEY

verticaleditions.com

THE LEGEND

THE STORY OF THE WORLD'S OLDEST PROFESSIONAL BOXER

STEVE WARD
WITH JOHN BRINDLEY

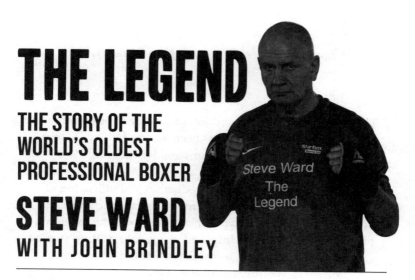

FOREWORD BY DANNY WILLIAMS

VERTICAL
editions

First published in the United Kingdom in 2021 by Vertical
Editions, Unit 41 Regency Court, Sheffield, S35 9ZQ

www.verticaleditions.com

Cover design by Sam Turner
Cover images by Richard Markham Photography

ISBN 9781908847249

A CIP catalogue record for this book
is available from the British Library

Printed and bound by Jellyfish
Print Solutions, Swanmore, Hants

*To my dad, Bernard James
Ward; my mum, Amy Ward; and
my wife Lucy; without whom there
would be no Steve Ward.
To the late Richard Longstaff,
for his contribution towards this
book, and Mark Waddingham,
inspiration for the multi
award-winning documentary*
Champ of Champs *by Keith Large.*

CONTENTS

INTRODUCTION

By Mark Waddingham, of Champs café

S teve Ward and his wife Lucy first walked into my café, which was situated on the A453 near East Midlands Airport, in 2014. My initial thought, as a very keen boxing fan, was: "Do I know you?"

"I bet you do!" he replied.

"Oh shit," I thought. "He's going to give me a slap!"

I asked if he was a boxer and he said I was on the right lines. When he told me his name, I had heard of him, but didn't know much about him. I thought he was winding me up when he said he was still fighting in his late fifties. But no!

I let him know Nigel Benn was one of my boxing heroes and asked if he could bring in a glove as a memento. A couple of weeks later, he came back with a signed glove of his own, and one signed by Nigel. And that was the start of our friendship. Steve and Lucy came in every other week after attending Donington Sunday Market and we chatted. He was officially the oldest active boxer in the world, his name was in the Guinness Book of World Records, and I found his story unreal.

Later, I lived in Thailand, the Philippines and Vietnam and while I was abroad, I met some sports fans from Nottingham in a bar. By coincidence, they put on the TV and it was Steve Ward, my amazing friend, fighting for a world title! I couldn't believe my eyes. When I returned home a couple of weeks later, I decided to dedicate the café to Steve – he WAS the Champ of Champs, in my eyes. I wasted no time tracking him down and that's what happened.

Steve brought in more and more memorabilia and the café grew and grew. It became one of the best known in the country and attracted a lot of well-known faces. They enjoyed looking at what we had put together, with many customers interested in Steve and his achievements. The café was laid out with WBA and WBC belts, pictures and posters, gloves, shorts and robes. We even had a life-size statue of the great Mike Tyson and I dedicated my blue Mazda to Steve 'The Legend' Ward.

Among the interested customers was Keith Large, a film producer and director. He was very interested in Steve. So, I put him in touch and his documentary *Champ of Champs* was up and running. Some scenes were filmed at the café and the documentary has won awards all over the world – Brazil, Mexico, India, America, Cannes Film Festival in France, Germany and Britain all included. It's been a great success. But this is a fantastic story.

The incredible thing is that, as I'm writing this, Steve Ward is still fighting. He told me a few months ago about another world title fight – the first ever being staged on a cruise ship. How great was that? Then he found out it was all an elaborate scam and his hopes were dashed.

All is revealed in this book. Once you pick it up, you won't be able to put it down. You're going to love reading about Steve Ward, a human being with a heart of gold. And a man I am proud to call my mate.

FOREWORD

By Danny Williams, WBC world heavyweight title contender

I was boxing in my mid-forties, and hating it, when a mutual friend told me about Steve Ward. He was still fighting in his sixties, as the oldest professional boxer in the world, because he wanted to – and still a real handful.

I'm in a good position to know how difficult that is. I would train properly, then be so tired I couldn't do anything for three or four days afterwards. My body was telling me I shouldn't be doing it and I've been quoted as saying I didn't just fear losing. I feared I could lose my life in the ring.

People know me as the boxer who knocked out Mike Tyson and fought Vitali Klitschko for the WBC world heavyweight title in 2004. But, in the last few years, I fought for only one reason – money. I wanted to ensure my daughters got a good education away from some of the problems I experienced.

I started to hate boxing, whilst still taking an interest in how others were doing. I really enjoyed meeting Steve face to face because I was in awe of what he has achieved in the sport, and I viewed footage of his fight with the German boxer Andreas Sidon in 2017. Here he was, in the ring with a serious heavyweight; someone I fought and lost to.

I saw for myself how good and fit Steve still was – he was six rounds up and only lost because of an injury. It was great to hear about him finally bowing out of boxing just before his 65th birthday with a victory that made him the first World Legends champion.

All boxers want to go out at the top – but very few of us do. Steve Ward achieved that. I also found out what a great bloke he is outside of the ring, and that is also very important.

Retirement is going to be difficult – big time. He has been boxing for a very long time and it becomes your life. I was going to say I hope he has a good woman to look after him, but now I know he has a lovely wife, Lucy – who is 18 years younger than him. What a bad boy!

It's 100 per cent true that not enough people know about Steve Ward. I hope his book sells well, because this is a fantastic story – and an inspiration to many. Now we've both retired, I hope to meet up with Steve soon. He's the man, trust me!

1

GIVEN A FIGHTING CHANCE

By Marcellus Baz, BEM, managing director of the Nottingham School of Boxing
Steve is the connection between the old Nottingham School of Boxing and the one I reopened in 2013 at a different venue. He helps others to relive their memories of those times. He is an inspiration, a role model, to young and older people alike. It's great he is in the Guinness Book of World Records as the world's oldest active professional boxer.
In the three or four years I have known him, he has helped with events promoting mental health and given us the benefit of his advice. His own achievements have been massive. He is a machine. People usually retire from boxing at half Steve's age.
I watched his fight for a world title in 2017 and he was doing really well until he suffered a heavy injury. He was going to retire but only Steve could have come back from that. I take my hat off to him.

My first fight was for life itself. "Your baby son is small, tiny and, to be blunt, he has a very slim chance," the doctor told Dad. "I suggest you go, see your wife, prepare her and yourself for the worst." I weighed less than six pounds.

Bernard Ward put his hand on the doctor's shoulder as

he prepared to walk away. "Listen, doctor," he said. "You're wrong. My lad will get through, he'll survive. He'll fight for his life, you watch!" My mum, Amy, was equally defiant. "He'll be right as rain," she said as she touched her new son's face. "He'll make it. I know it."

Born on August 12, 1956, at Nottingham General Hospital, I made it through the night and, after the usual seven days in hospital, was allowed home to the small newsagents Dad ran in Hyson Green, part of the fast-growing city of Nottingham.

Dad was born and bred in St Ann's, Nottingham, and worked as a newsagent all his life. He and his brother had a fearsome reputation as local hard men. And, if there was no one else to fight, they would fight each other! He had met and married Amy, a strong-willed Scot and policewoman, a few years earlier, and in the most unusual circumstances.

Dad had been married before Mum came into his life. After his wife died, Dad became very withdrawn and unhappy. He didn't want to go anywhere and was getting worse and worse. Then one day Edward Martin came in from the shop next door and shouted for him. Smelling gas, he kept the front door open and rushed into the back, where he found Dad with his head in the oven. Immediately he called 999 for an ambulance and the young woman, who took that call, was so intrigued and worried that she called into the shop two or three days later to find out how this 'Bernard Ward' was. That woman was Mum, and the rest is history. They became friends and later married.

Dad's shop was like Arkwright's in Ronnie Barker's *Open All Hours* – packed with stuff. Only Dad, despite his failing eyesight, could have known where everything was like the back of his hand. Mum was a 'fighter' of a different kind.

She gained the respect of her police colleagues for being willing to jump into the middle of brawls when the pubs emptied on Saturday nights. Male and female newcomers alike were placed with her to learn the ropes and see if they had the guts to do the job. She was back on the beat within a year of my birth, as we needed her wage to help pay the bills.

I soon grew to an average size and was paraded around the close-knit community with pride by Dad. Modern for his times, he thought nothing of feeding, changing and taking me for a walk in the pram and my first childhood memory was of the family dog, an English bullmastiff called Hamma. I had a hand in the naming because I struggled to say 'Sandy' and 'Hamma' seemed more appropriate. One day he bit me, so I reacted and bit his tail. We were the best of mates after that. I was three or four at the most, but Hamma never showed his teeth to me again.

I have very fond memories of the shop and, of course, Dad. I remember the smell of Gold Leaf tobacco, sweet aroma of jars of confectionery and the shift workers Dad caught by opening up at 3am. The smell of hops from workers at Shipstones brewery was awful, and visitors who made soap at the Gerard's soap factory made my young eyes water.

Dad had poor eyesight – he told me he had arthritis in his eyes – but a keen sense of hearing, and I spent much of my childhood watching him in that shop. He recognised customers by their voices or the way they walked in. I began to cheek him, thinking he couldn't see to give me a back-hander. I was wrong. He knew where I was from my voice and gave me a good clip round the ear.

From the age of six, I helped Dad by dressing the shop

window, something I developed a flair for and very useful in my working life. I usually swapped things around weekly to give the public a taste of what we had inside, but I learnt an important lesson when the shop suffered a smash and grab. I made the mistake of putting expensive watches towards the front and local lads helped themselves. The illuminated Durex machine was also popular but stayed firmly in place!

Dad's other passion got him and our little family our first taste of fame. He loved all animals, but mynah birds were top of the list. He spent hours teaching those intelligent birds how to speak, and our Charlie became British champion. He knew over 300 words! That got me and Mum an invite to London for the popular children's TV show, *Blue Peter*.

I was about nine, it was my first appearance on live TV and it didn't go to plan. Charlie talked constantly on the train and in the taxi from the station – but, as soon as we went through the studio doors, he shut up and we couldn't get a word out of him. Unfortunately, Dad wasn't with us, because he was minding the shop. Back in the taxi, we couldn't stop Charlie talking! I've still got a black and white photo of *Blue Peter* dog Petra and the pups. Presenters Valerie Singleton and Christopher Trace and producer Biddy Baxter signed it on the back.

People travelled from far and wide to ask Dad how to teach the birds to speak. He worked out a way using a tape recorder. I even witnessed Charlie serving in the shop – he was that good. A shift worker and regular customer asked for his 'usual' and Charlie answered: "10 Park Drive". The man didn't realise he was talking to the bird and was still none the wiser when Dad appeared with the cigarettes.

Another bird, Jimmy, was a bit near the knuckle. He wolf-whistled at women and squawked: "Show us your knickers!" One day waiting for the newspapers, the bird got me a slap around the face – and a good one, at that – from a woman who thought I had made the cheeky comment. That was funny in a way, but what happened next caused us real trouble with the brewery. Big dray horses, two at a time pulling a ton or more of ale barrels, came by the shop. Jimmy spotted them from the shop window and shouted: "Go on, giddy up, go faster."

Poor blokes were trying with all their strength to slow the horses down, with barrels flying everywhere. God knows how no one was badly injured. The manager of Shipstones then begged Dad to put Jimmy out of sight at certain times of the day.

Dad's love of creatures extended to us having three birds, a dog, a small monkey and a chimpanzee. But even his expertise couldn't keep everything under control. We got Cheeta, the chimp, from an Asian man working at Gerard's. I took him on walks in his red bib and braces up Radford Road and one day, Cheeta climbed up a lamppost. Folk walked by whilst I stood there, arm in the air and feet off the ground, clinging desperately to his lead, until Cheeta decided to come down!

Another time, he climbed onto a parked builder's van. It began to move as I tried to haul Cheeta back down. The driver never noticed what was happening. Then, there was the unfortunate incident with a nearby café owner's aggressive German Shepherd. The dog growled and barked outside our shop door; it sounded more like a wolf than a dog. Cheeta jumped in, and the dog came out second best.

The owner contacted the police, who knew the dog and

were very understanding. They gave us a quiet warning to keep our monkey in order, but that wasn't why we decided to let Cheeta go. Chimps revert to their wild state later in life and all of us could have been at risk. So, Dad took him to the arboretum and, from there, our former pet was last seen at Twycross Zoo.

Mum and Dad were sticklers for bad language, and anyone swearing in the shop or on the street knew about it. I had to stop myself laughing when we all went to see mynah birds at Nottingham arboretum. Dad had been looking forward to it for weeks and although he was no big head, he liked people to know he was an expert. He pointed at one bird, explaining what species it was from looking at its paler neck band and the way it sat, when suddenly it shrieked at the top of its voice: "Fuck off four eyes, fuck off four eyes!"

You should have seen Dad's face... he was bright red and fuming. He turned to Mum and said: "Come on, we're leaving. What a foulmouthed bird." It still makes me smile thinking about it now. Even a hint of a giggle and he would have gone mad. As it was, I missed out on an ice cream. All my parents talked about for the rest of the day was "that disgusting bird".

When I was about eight, Dad asked me to walk him to Strothers, the opticians, on Radford Road, about a mile from the newsagent shop. He was there so often they knew him by his first name. He needed glasses which had inch-thick lenses for both eyes. I was on the stairs whilst he talked with Mum back home. His eyesight would get worse, he said, until he eventually went blind. I wish I hadn't overheard that.

I began my education at Scotholme Primary School on

Beaconsfield Street in Nottingham, where I learnt more important lessons than English and maths. I stood my ground and fought! This was back in the age of corporal punishment with the strap, cane, slipper and even wooden or metal rulers. I went to school every morning wondering who would hit me today. It was a toss-up between the bullies and the teachers. I hate using the word to describe a woman, but the headmistress, Miss Plowright, was a total bitch. She hated me from the second we met. And the feeling was mutual!

My first friends became mates for life. Stafford McKen and Neville Hamilton, both from the Afro-Caribbean community, were targets for bullies because of racism and bigotry. I was picked on because I was small, one of the youngest, and comparatively poor. Bullying is about someone deciding you don't fit in. I didn't stand up to them at first and learnt a lifelong lesson: do nothing and you get a good kicking!

I was on the receiving end of kicks, cruel names and teasing as Scotholme became a living nightmare. Walking at night, acting as a guide for Dad, they shouted "puff boy" as Dad put his hand on my shoulder. That hurt both our feelings. Top of the list of school bullies was Grenville Bramley, who told me to steal sweets and cigarettes from Dad's shop or get a good hiding. No way would I rob my own family, so I took the beating. Telling the teachers was no good and Miss Plowright said it was my own fault. This went on until I was nine, when I decided enough was enough.

Things came to a head in the school toilets when I was washing my hands. Bramley came in with five of his mates and I was shitting myself. He started with the names, then having a go at Dad. "Why does he walk with his hand on your shoulder?" he said. "Bet he likes little boys." I said he was nearly blind, but it made no difference. He bragged to his mates about how he was going to beat me up.

Bramley was big and strong but turning his back on me was a mistake. *Bang!* A hard punch caught him on his face, jaw and ear. His fat legs buckled as he slumped to the floor. I kicked him in the balls when he got up, and he cried like a dog. His mates stood with mouths open and wide eyes. Neither they, nor Bramley, came near me for a while.

That got me a long lecture on 'bullying' and the cane from Miss Plowright. But I stood my ground. "You can't hurt me," I said when she hit me on the palm of my hand, and it stung like mad. When she hit me again, I said: "That still doesn't hurt." It was killing me, but I had stopped being a victim and God, it felt good. Mum and Dad were very angry when I got home. Mum said: "Get your coat on," and off we went back to the school. She walked straight into Miss Plowright's office and, after a few choice words, Mum punched her on the chin. The headmistress fell backwards, landing on top of her desk, stuff flying everywhere.

When there had been thefts of sweets from coat pockets, I got wrongly accused of being the culprit. After Mr. Curtain had taken over as headmaster, he ordered me into the office and, without listening to anything I said, gave me a whack with the strap. I didn't wait for a second one; I grabbed my coat and rushed out the door. This time I was crying – it really hurt. Again, Mum took me back to school and warned Mr. Curtain that, if he laid his hands on me in the future, it would be the last thing he ever did.

The other person in the school to get bullied as much as me was a small slip of a girl called Wendy Kirk. Mum was convinced it was because we came from poor backgrounds and made her feelings clear to Mr. Curtain. But school wasn't all that bad; it was there I met my first 'love', Faye Goodwin. She was a beautiful girl and everyone's hands shot up in the air for the role to play the spider in the school play when Faye became Little Miss Muffet. My dream came true when I got the part.

Dad noted my reaction to the bullying and had been talking about taking me to a boxing club. But, when it happened for real, it was still a big surprise. This particular night I walked home from school with my two mates Neville and Stafford before Dad said: "Your tea is on the table, then we are off out." I threw my food down my neck with excitement, but he wouldn't tell me where we were going.

Taking in the sights of the city as I guided Dad through Nottingham's streets was amazing. It's all glass and chrome today, but it was so nice back then, with the smells of spice and fish from the small shops and the side street markets selling anything and everything.

Loads of folk shouted hello as I kept Dad safe, warning him of kerbs, lampposts and dog muck. Of course, I didn't know where I was heading myself. We navigated by a few landmarks, including the old John Player tobacco factory, and eventually landed up at a row of garages near the Boulevard Hotel.

Dad said the last garage should be open and told me to walk up the stairs. We walked into a changing room and from the old horsehair boxing gloves hanging up in the corner and the upright scales that were standing on the floor, I realised this must be the boxing club my dad had been threatening to take me to. I felt very apprehensive. I was nine years old and couldn't see anyone my size or age. All the other lads were five or six years older or grown men. What was I doing here?

Dad went up to Arthur Mason, who ran the Nottingham School of Boxing with Harold Bamford. "I have brought my son, Steve," he said. When Harold and the others walked in, it became clear they knew Dad from the paper shop. "I would like you to toughen Steve up," Dad continued. "He is having problems with the bigger lads and bullies at school."

I was taken into the end room and given my first task – learning to skip. There were five or six other lads in there, as I found out skipping was far from easy. I didn't think I would get the hang of it. Then I did some exercises along with a group of about 20 others, including adults. I did my best to copy them and not look out of place.

Harold showed me what to do whilst Arthur was the taskmaster. Everything was done correctly. After about 20 minutes, I was introduced to boxing gloves. They nearly came up to my elbows. I was told how to put my hands up in defence, place my feet in the right place and jab. For two or three months, that's as far as my boxing lessons went. They were tedious and repetitive. What was all this about?

Dad asked after our first visit if I'd enjoyed it. My answer was emphatic: "No." The next day, when I got up for school and came down into the shop, Dad pointed at a photograph of me and told a customer: "This is my son. Look at him and remember his face. One day he will be heavyweight champion of the world!" He had total faith and knew he had found the perfect sport for me.

We started going there on Tuesday and Thursday nights from six o'clock until about half seven or eight o'clock, and on Sunday from 10 o'clock until noon. We had no transport, so it meant a five-mile walk each way. Arthur asked if I could run, I said yes, and I joined in a three-mile run round the Forest recreation ground, which houses the Goose Fair. That was until I got better at it and the run was made longer.

Running was the first part of life at the boxing club I enjoyed, but I still didn't like the training. My early thoughts were that it wasn't for me, but I did it because I had no option. What Dad said, I normally did. That's how it worked in our family. After a month, Dad asked if I was liking it a bit more. "No," was again my answer.

The work I did at the club increased slowly – that's how boxing is. You have to learn one step at a time. First, I was introduced to the swinging bag which I whacked with both hands, followed by the stand-ball, a punchball on a big steel stand, and the speed-ball fixed to the wall.

I was beginning to get to know the place. The two trainers couldn't have been more different but were both fantastic blokes. Harold, a window cleaner, was quiet and someone I could talk to; Arthur, a builder, was exceptionally loud and shouted at everyone.

I was the baby of the group. And that got me the ultimate job of emptying the wee bucket at the end of training. Because I didn't complain, I went up in the estimation of both Arthur and Harold. The other lads didn't say much to me but always kept me in line if I did something wrong. I wasn't making great friends, but at least I wasn't being bullied.

After two or three months, it was time to spar. The idea was for us all to do two rounds each. When my name was called, I found myself with a problem. There was nothing I could do against older lads, who were fit and fast. Dad had told the trainers to add me to the group to toughen me up. I was sparring with lads up to 15 years old. They were told to hold back and not flatten me but, if my gloves dropped, they gave me a good whack.

Within seconds, my nose was bleeding and I went home that night with a black eye and a wobbly tooth as well. Mum was so upset she asked what on earth had happened. I couldn't stand boxing at this point. It was getting worse and worse. I couldn't see the benefit. Dad took me boxing because I was getting bullied at school. I was still getting bullied there, and I was now also being bullied at the boxing club as well!

Just as I was beginning to find my feet, I had an accident at school. It happened because a prat of a teacher insisted on sending me up the monkey climber hanging from the ceiling in the school hall. I begged him not to do so because I had a fear of heights from an incident a couple of years previously, when I froze so badly after climbing up the side of the shop and the building next door that the fire brigade had to be called to rescue me. But the teacher wouldn't take no for an answer and dragged me to the rope.

Up I went slowly, shaking and with sweat dripping off me. I took the teacher's word not to look down but, as I tried to touch the ceiling, my other arm gave way through sheer fear and down I plunged like a sack of shit. Had I landed on my head, I could have been killed as there were no safety mats. Thankfully, I landed on my shoulder. The teacher went as white as a sheet, knowing he was in trouble, and the pain told me the damage was bad.

The school nurse phoned Mum, who was livid. Within minutes she was at the school, demanding a full explanation, and I knew it was going to end in tears. The teacher lied by claiming the accident was my fault for 'fooling around' and Mr. Curtain backed him up. That was red rag to a bull. Mum again made her point very forcefully.

After an agonising bus journey to the children's hospital, I was told my shoulder was dislocated. The way they pulled and manipulated it back in place is something I won't ever forget. I was in a sling for a week and banned from heavy exercise for three. I also had to deal with a familiar problem as Grenville plagued me by getting me to hand over my crisp money instead of getting a hiding. Time and time again I reluctantly gave in.

Now I was nearly 11 and growing up fast. "The money is in my pocket and it is staying there," I told the bully. I knew what was coming, as Grenville stood there with a couple of lads behind him. But I took the fight to him. I hit him with four punches, all on the face, and stopped him dead in his tracks. Then I knocked him off his feet with a big right hand.

"The money stays in my pocket from today!" I told him. I had seen off Grenville, the school bully, for good.

2

THE LOVE OF BOXING GROWS

Having fought off the bullies at primary school, I had to start all over again at 'big school' after winning the battle to go to Ellis Guilford, a secondary modern on Bar Lane, Basford. My parents were delighted I passed my 11-plus exam and Dad talked about Forest Fields Grammar School. It was this and that, the best place and full of children from good backgrounds. I didn't want to know for two reasons – my mates Neville and Stafford were going to Ellis Guilford and I didn't want to go to 'posh school' because I wasn't a snob.

Boy, I fell out with Dad about it, but Mum saved the day when she pointed out the cost of the kit. We struggled long and hard to afford clothing for Ellis Guilford; the other school would have been out of our reach, particularly with the shop on its knees and Mum wanting to retire soon.

My parents scraped together enough money for the basic uniform of bottle green blazer, black trousers, black lace-up shoes, white shirt, bottle green and gold striped tie and a cap, which was optional and I only wore once. When they couldn't afford to buy from the expensive school suppliers, they found alternatives from the army and navy stores. Their hardships however were nothing compared with what I faced for wearing it. Even the teachers said: "What have you come to school as this week, Ward... soldier or sailor?" One week I was wearing a Royal Navy officer's shirt, the next a thick overcoat fit for a Russian admiral.

At the boxing club, I sparred with the likes of Tommy Anderton, Jim Cannon and Tony Hoffman, all big lads and good fighters, and even David Needham, a local hero I'll be saying a lot more about later. All gave me tips and helped me develop. Then came my big moment. I was told I was eligible for my first fight, arranged on my 11th birthday. My thought was: "What do I want to fight for?" The idea gave me a lump in my throat. I really didn't want to do it.

Harold told me a bit about my opponent a couple of weeks before my big night. "He's local and a tasty lad, fast and good on his feet," he said. "You will need to work hard on him, son." I then put everything into my training regime over that next fortnight. I was at the club as soon as the school bell went on a Tuesday and Thursday and out running on Sunday with trainer Lionel Preston and the lads.

I had this focus – don't ask me where it comes from – but I had it aged 11 and it's been with me ever since. I had a fight on my mind and nothing was going to get in the way. Mum and Dad spotted it and backed me up. They told my mates I was staying in when they called wanting me to go out with them. All that mattered was my fight.

It was at Daybrook Working Men's Club in Arnold in 1967, and our first task was how to get there. Mum didn't drive and Dad's eyesight meant he couldn't either. Taxis were too expensive but, luckily, we managed to get a lift part of the way, then catch a bus that dropped us about a mile from the venue. Mum and Dad had bought tickets but, walking into the club, I didn't know what to do. What next? I was taken to the changing room where I recognised faces from the Nottingham School of Boxing. They were mostly 12 and 13-year-olds with some fighting experience. I felt on my own and out of my depth.

One lad asked me who I was fighting and I said I didn't know. Harold said I was third or fourth fight on, so I asked about my opponent. The first I knew about Paul Ironmonger was seeing his name in the programme Harold brought to me. I found out this was also Paul's first fight and asked a few questions. No, he wasn't bigger than me, he was roughly the same size and weight. Arthur said it was time to weigh in, a new one on me. All I remember is that both of us were exactly the same weight.

I had a grudge against Paul Ironmonger even before I set eyes on him. It was because of him I had suffered black eyes, crooked teeth and bloody noses over the past two years of training at the club. And he was why I hadn't been allowed to go out with my friends. All good reasons to give him a hard time!

It was time to put my kit on. Mum and Dad had scraped up £7 to buy me some Winnit black leather boxing boots and the club supplied the shorts – black and maroon three-quarter length that came within six inches of my boots.

Amateur boxing nights meant a lot back then. A crowd of about 200 had gathered, all local so everyone knew each other. Out I went for my fight. The lights above the ring looked like those you see over a snooker table – very bright with smoke and with cigarette smoke drifting up to them.

I was wrapped in a gown as I walked towards the ring. Arthur jumped over the apron and lifted up the ropes for me to clamber in. My first thought was: "Oh God, what am I doing here?"

I recognised some faces in the crowd through boxing and spotted Mum and Dad near the front. Mum was telling Dad 'He's in the ring now'. Mum smiled, clapped and told Dad what was happening throughout the fight. I nodded shyly at them. Nobody wants to acknowledge their parents too much in public.

Ironmonger looked mean, but that didn't worry me. He could look as mean as he liked; I was going to beat the crap out of him. We were announced and there was a lot of cheering for Paul. "He must be good, he's very popular," I thought. But that was nothing compared with when my name was called – the place went ballistic. I was the local lad, after all. The fight was over three one and a half minute rounds – each of which seemed like 20 minutes.

More frightening was the referee – a Scottish guy called Jock. "Lads, come to the centre now!" he barked. One of the trainers followed me. "I want a good clean fight. When told to fight, you will; if one of you goes down, the other goes to a neutral corner. Break when I say break. No low shots or you'll be disqualified, do you understand?" We nodded, touched gloves and went back to our corners.

Harold was in one ear telling me to hold my nerve; Arthur in the other going through how to fight round one – move my feet, watch my guard. I looked at the crowd, still wondering if I really wanted to be there in my head. Harold smeared Vaseline over my eyebrows and Arthur told me to pace myself. He should have saved his breath!

When the bell sounded and the trainers left the ring, the referee made us touch gloves again out of respect. After fighting with myself in my own head, I now had no fear; I was calm. I knew I could do it. Dad had told me not to be nervous and I wasn't. From the first bell, there was no pacing about it. It was all hell for leather, get him before he gets me stuff. No style, no tactics, no headguards. We must have thrown 100 punches each. But, from the first punch he caught me with, I realised this was why I was here – to do a job.

Back in my corner, Arthur welcomed me to competitive boxing. "What the hell are you doing?" he asked. "You aren't moving forward; you're letting him come to you. Get your legs open, sit up, breathe. He's got you; you lost that one, get out there and work him." I turned to Harold to ask his opinion. "Ask me later," he replied. I knew Arthur was pushing me, but thought I'd been so poor I needed to step it up.

Forward, forward, forward were the words going round in my head as I came out for round two. I started to get Ironmonger on the back foot and kids don't know how to fight like that. There were more tactics too. Now it was all about jabs, saving energy for the third and final round. We were more careful, working each other out. His reach, my reach, his jab, my jab. I gave Ironmonger a bloody nose. I saw the referee looking to step in as I was banging away.

"That's better," said Arthur, careful not to give me too much praise. "Now, let your right hand go!" Legs open, sitting up, breathing, lungs burning, arms like heavy steel pipes. Arthur went on about footwork and doing this and that; Harold, calm as ever, talked slowly, looked straight into my eyes and greased me up.

Out I went. Do or die! We touched gloves for the final round, then bang! The bees' nest of the first round was back, with tactics out of the window. I took Ironmonger by surprise with a right hand. I saw him looking at me, then down he fell. I went to a neutral corner as the referee started the count. To his credit, Paul got to his feet. The ref checked his eyes to see if he was still fit enough to carry on. Then he stopped the fight. He waved his arms, turned to Paul's corner and said: "He's done, no more."

I was announced as the winner. The referee held my hand up and the first thing I did was go over to Paul and say: "Well done!" We hugged each other – it was pure instinct, no prompting from our corners. That's the respect that runs through boxing. I shook his hand and his trainer's and went back to my corner. Mum and Dad were on their feet clapping and shouting.

"Well done lad, good right hand," Harold said. Then I turned to Arthur, telling him I had done it. Rubbing me down with a towel, he said: "Don't be a cocky fucker then, you still need to work on your feet." I knew my place. He was right. I had won a fight, that's all, I still needed to improve and keep my feet on the ground.

That's why Arthur Mason and Harold Bamford were so good as trainers. They made us into good all-round humans, not just fighters. The respect I had for both, and the lad I had just beaten, stayed with me. I wasn't going to show off in front of my defeated opponent – that would be me one day!

Back in the changing room, my mind turned to other things. "Excuse me, Harold, don't I get a sandwich?" He passed me a raffle ticket and I went to the bar. It was a voucher for a sandwich, crisps and a bottle of pop. I also got a small trophy for winning, but the sandwich and crisps were more important. Mum and Dad were as proud as punch as they looked at my trophy, the first prize I ever won in boxing.

I walked home to Hyson Green with my parents, with

Dad's hand as usual on my shoulder. I was reminded how much time and effort Dad had put in to make that night possible – coming with me twice a week training, the kit and the expense our family could have done without. Dad asked me how I felt now I had won the fight. "I hate it," I said. It was an honest answer, even though I was pleased for myself and my parents the evening had gone so well.

I didn't like the training and would have done anything to get out of my regular visits to the club. I was a busy boy – Mum insisted that because I was going boxing for Dad, I should do something for her. That's how my piano lessons came about, although almost everything in my life was re-volving around boxing. It took me a fair while to shrug off my dislike of boxing. Even after five or six fights – all wins – all I could think about was getting hurt and that I was training whilst my friends were having fun. Even when I got the bike I wanted, the gift was designed so I could get to training quicker and earlier.

I didn't like going to the boxing shows because of the smoke. With the spotlight shining down at the venues, it felt like walking into a film of smog. Both my parents were smokers – Dad being a chain smoker – and I hate that smell of smoke to this day. It makes me feel ill. But eventually I started to realise that there was an upside to boxing after all, because it kept me on the right side of Dad.

He was beginning to live his second childhood through my boxing. Denied some of life's pleasures due to his fading eyesight, he was finding enjoyment again through me. My increased confidence also helped me with the school bullies and I could run like lightning. Yet, even after 15 fights or so, I would have stopped if I had the choice.

Dad was keen on me standing up for myself. If anyone

hit me, I should fight back. But I wasn't going to let anyone have the satisfaction of getting in that first hit. I got myself into trouble at school when a girl got me by the throat, digging her long nails into my neck and drawing blood. I had to do something as I was nearly blacking out, but my dad's advice was going through my mind: "Never hit a girl." So I headbutted her instead. I knew it was very easy to step over the line and become a bully myself, even though I'd been fighting the same thing all my life. Fewer and fewer people were mucking about with me. I had a couple of mates without being part of the in-crowd, and that was fine. All I wanted was to be left alone.

Then came a highly significant moment in my life as I refused to be the victim anymore and took charge of my own life. In the school gym a lad called Steve hit me for no reason. He smashed me on the head with a badminton racket, to roars of laughter from about 30 lads watching. As I walked out to cries of "chicken" I could feel something happening with my head. I looked in the mirror in the changing room and saw a lump the size of an egg coming up on the side of my eye. I asked myself: "What would Dad want me to do about this?" And I knew the answer.

Steve was still holding the racket when I walked back over to him. I punched him three times – and once more for luck, as he was about to hit the floor. Reaching down to grab him, I felt a pull on my ear. It was Mr. Acclam, the gym and sports teacher. "Get back into the changing room, you bully," he shouted. Me, a bully? I showed him my eye, but he didn't want to know. I thought he was going to cane or strap me or hand me in to the headmaster for the same punishment. Instead, he told me to wait whilst he went into another room.

Out he came and threw a pair of boxing gloves at me. They came up to my elbows but, unknown to Mr. Acclam, I was very familiar with them. Back in the gym, between 300 and 400 lads and girls were packed in, sensing entertainment ahead.

"I'm going to teach you some manners and not to be a bully," he said. "Now put your hands up!" He started jabbing at me. He hadn't a clue that, at the age of 12, I already had more than three years of boxing experience. I used my skills to parry his punches with my gloves or avoid them altogether. Then I decided to hit back. A little shaken, he straightened up and came back at me – jab, jab, jab. This was my chance. I landed three punches that produced a little trickle of blood from his nose, then a fourth that caused his nose to explode. Mr. Acclam fell down on his knees and the place erupted.

Slowly my gym teacher got to his feet, wiping the blood onto his gloves and shrugging his shoulders. Then he came out with a line that had me laughing inside. "Now let that be a lesson to you, Ward," he said, as he walked out. Happily, for me, there were no repercussions from the boxing lesson I had handed out to him and I particularly looked forward to seeing Dad when I got back home. "There's something you haven't asked me for a while, Dad," I said. "I love boxing!" I had genuinely changed. The sport that had caused me more hurt and pain was now proving very good for me.

Not only was I standing up for myself at school, but I was also gaining friends at the boxing club. We had become a very close-knit group and our friendship and comradeship were second to none. We went hell for leather at each other when we were sparring but wouldn't let anyone outside of the group hurt any one of us. We bled together and laughed together and the mutual affection between us was unreal.

One example was at the Goose Fair site when a group of four lads picked on Terry Hodson, who was our flagship. They suddenly found 15 of us more than capable of knocking the hell out of them. I knew then that boxing wasn't just an individual sport and a useful life skill, but a fraternity. In boxing if you make a friend, it's not for weeks, it's for life. Whenever one of us was boxing, the rest came to support. I stayed at that boxing club until I was 18 and, after those early days, I enjoyed every minute.

Sadly, Dad didn't have much time to bask in my success because he was suffering from life-changing events of his own. The shop had been losing money for years. Larger shops had opened in the Hyson Green area and could undercut our prices and although Mum was working in the shop as much as possible, Dad's eyesight was fading fast. To make things worse, friends – or so-called friends – took advantage of Dad's condition, saying he short-changed them by a shilling or a pound at a time. But, in truth, they knew he couldn't see, and they used that to steal from him. This upsets me more than 50 years later when I still think about it.

Mum said she would give up her job with the police to help Dad full time but it made little difference. The shop was on its knees, losing money hand over fist. I filled in as best I could, collecting the paper money on a Sunday morning after my run with the boxing club. Hyson Green was full of working girls, or prostitutes, who always paid up, even giving me a good Christmas tip. I had a lot of respect for them, and still do. Unlike our so-called friends, they never robbed our family.

When I was 12, it was clear the shop had to go. Dad's

vision was so bad he was provided with a guide dog and just before Mum and Dad decided to shut up shop, disaster struck. It was the one day I didn't observe the golden rule in our house of not leaving anything on the stairs.

I abandoned my toy car when I heard a knock on the door. Then came the crash. Dad had gone flying and was at the bottom of the stairs in agony. He must have gone up in the air and fallen like a stone. I still blame myself for all that followed.

Dad suffered terrible pain in his lower back for the next few months. Hospital appointments and private treatments followed, but nothing seemed to improve and other problems surfaced. He had a swollen stomach, becoming constipated one day and having diarrhoea the next. He lost weight and was very tired, causing Mum to worry. As prospective buyers called, Mum had to close the shop to care for Dad. The situation was pushing her to the limit.

Doctors told Dad it was stomach cancer. I found out later. I think they needed to come to terms with it themselves before landing the bombshell on me. To make things worse, the bastard who bought the shop ripped Mum and Dad off by underpaying by £1,000. That put us on the breadline, and I mean breadline when we moved to a small two-bedroom house on Hazelwood Road, Hyson Green.

Mum took on a cleaning job at Shipstones brewery and continued to care for Dad when she got home. He still made it to training with me twice a week but was getting worse by the day. I felt terrible for him. After all the work he put in, countless hours behind that counter from three in the morning until six at night, he came out with nothing. Mum and Dad lost it all, and it hurt.

He was a proud man who saw himself as head of the family and the provider. Now he was in very ill health, with no shop, no job and little money. It made me determined it would never happen to me. I would do all I could to have a good life and the good things that go with it. It was a big lesson for a 13-year-old.

It was then that we had our one and only family holiday. This wasn't possible when the shop was open seven days a week and Dad would never trust it to others. Going to Mablethorpe for a week was a special time, although I wasn't very keen about going along with everything Mum and Dad wanted to do. It wasn't long before I wanted to go running as a break from their walks through the town, but I'm pleased we spent that precious time together.

I have mixed feelings about my time at Ellis Guilford School. I would say it was 75 per cent good and 25 per cent bad. I made good mates, had girlfriends on and off and did what all lads do at that age, including looking for trouble. It says something about my school life that, despite all the bullying and hassle, I only played truant once. That was for a special reason – a *Radio One* event at the Commodore Hotel one lunchtime, which left the school half empty.

If that confused headmaster Mr. Green, known as Dembo, fights between prefects and the second, third and fourth years were more of an issue. They came about because of prefects throwing their weight around. Eventually the younger pupils fought back. Regular battles followed, with the younger ones using cricket bats, chair legs and anything else they could get their hands on. It was like St Trinian's, with teachers losing control. It was no coincidence a police station was built next door.

I put most of my time into boxing, partly to escape from what was happening at home, and I learnt more about being an adult than my mates. Their worlds seemed so perfect. Most had good families, money and the chance to do what they wanted when they wanted. I had to be a helper and provider for my parents. Today they call it being a carer; I call it being a son.

I left school three days before my 15th birthday with no qualifications. I needed a job more than education and the day after my birthday I started work at Lennon Brothers, a warehouse in George Street, Nottingham. It was hard going but I enjoyed it. I was paid three pounds, 10 shillings a week – three pounds went to my parents, the rest to me. They needed it.

Because they noticed my flair for window displays, I got promotion to become company showman. It was a good job, but I was always looking for more money. At 17, I went to Earnshaws paint factory. Now that was good money – £9 per week. Six to my parents and three for me.

Unfortunately, that didn't last long. Mr. Ganney, the owner, spoke to everyone like dog shit on his shoe. He didn't know how to be nice. I endured hours of him going on about me not doing my job, calling me idle this and idle that, until I lost it and pushed him into the paint vats. He stood there, dripping from head-to-toe in white paint and screaming the factory down. I was every name under the sun. He was about to sack me when I said I had already written out my notice. I thought it was justice when the factory burnt down that weekend.

Dad, though, was far from impressed. He was worried about my good money drying up and the family being unable to make ends meet, and it caused an almighty row. Neither of my parents were greedy nor held onto money as if it was the be all and end all, but Dad wanted me to give him £8 a week and have £1 for myself. I thought £6 was reasonable and refused.

Mum was caught in the middle as pride won the day. Neither of us backed down and that meant we barely spoke to each other for two years. We were living under the same roof and not speaking. God, it was awful. I wish I could go back and say: "Sorry, take it all." It was only money and didn't really matter.

Instead, I was 17 and the king of the world. I knew it all, was always right and everyone else was stupid. That cost me two years with a man I loved and respected. To go from being so close, hand on shoulder and always there no matter what, to not speaking and avoiding each other at all costs was heartbreaking.

I soon found a new job with one of the city's largest employers, Raleigh Cycles, working on the production line and going on to piecework. But even this failed to thaw the situation at home. I did a lot and got paid a lot. I was put on the section dealing with handlebars and pedals. I was quick, too quick. At one point I was earning £40 a week and that's when the trouble started.

Bosses thought I was fiddling and called in time and motion to watch me. They found out I was telling the truth, but my speed caused problems with the other workers. They didn't like being told they were slow and having me held up as an example of a good worker. The union threatened to bring everyone out on strike. Imagine what the bosses thought. They gave me eight weeks' pay at top rate before letting me go. I was disappointed because I liked the job and got on with just about everyone.

Mum took it very well. She laughed and said: "Don't worry son, this has happened so something better will come your way." That was Mum, always calm and never letting anything get the better of her. That's why she was such a good policewoman, and she was right. A week later I got a new job at a dye works called Weldon and Wilkinson. The staff were mainly women and, whilst other men chatted them up, I got down to the hard graft. It was soon spotted and I was promoted to chargehand. I was on big, big money for a kid of nearly 19, bringing home £58 a week. I loved the work and got on with everyone. I looked forward to going to work in the morning.

A long day's work was followed by boxing training three nights a week, plus a run every Sunday morning, and my reputation was growing within the amateur boxing community of Nottingham. More fights came my way, with opponents designed to test my skills and push me to my limits. Mostly, I overcame them with ease. Arthur and Harold knew I was close to the top of the amateur ranks. I was part of the national amateur and county teams and talked of as a future professional. There was some time in my teenage life for social fun as I saved up money to go out to the nightclub, Nottingham Palais, and it was there, when I was 17, I had another learning experience.

I was with a group of friends and one of them, Steve, had got himself into trouble with another bunch of lads. He was in a panic, saying someone was threatening to stab him. He hid behind me whilst his enemy asked whether I was Steve's friend and accused him of doing something I knew he hadn't done.

He was threatening to cut Steve's fucking tabs off and, as his friend, mine as well. This was getting serious, so I tried to ease a girl I was talking with out of the firing line. I moved Steve out of the way and took a step back, inviting the guy to move towards me. Then I clobbered him with a right hand straight under his chin. He fell to the floor with, everyone shouting: "Fight, fight..."

Staff closed in and I explained I had hit him because he had a knife. He and his friends were shown the door, but that wasn't the end of the evening. When we were about to go home, we noticed a dozen of them waiting for us. I alerted the club manager and he phoned the police. They moved the gang on so we could go home safely.

But what about the following week? I felt sure that they would be waiting for us. So, I rounded up around 100 of my friends in Hyson Green and Radford who were happy to support me. But surprisingly, the Eastwood gang never showed. I did bump into the main guy a couple of years later, walking across Maid Marion Way, and I wasn't bothered or frightened by him. I reminded him he had threatened to cut my tabs off, and he soon scuttled off.

3

SHATTERED DREAMS

By Kate Allsop, former directly elected Mayor of Mansfield
I have known Steve for many years. he really is a legend in his own
lifetime. A boxing hero and inspiration to so many people, our
paths crossed many times when I was directly elected Mayor of
Mansfield. I saw first-hand a giant of a man, who can light up a
room with his charisma.
Steve has endless stories to tell. how many men do we know who
are in the Guinness Book of World Records not once, but several
times? You will read in his book about his dedication to fitness
and determination to win, but you will also get a feel for a genu-
ine, really nice guy who would do anything for you.

Turning professional is many a young boxer's dream. For me, it almost became a nightmare. Being an honest guy, I will take some of it on the chin. I could have done better had my attitude been spot on. The rest was beyond my control. The death of my dad, my main inspiration to box, knocked me sideways and had a big impact on my life. I also lost my love for boxing as I left behind a sport and found myself in a business where the fighters all too often come last.

Boxers are taken in by visions of a glamorous world and the possibility of becoming millionaires almost overnight.

In my day very few made it big and many more fell flat on their arses. Without money or big sponsors behind you, it was very difficult. As for me, I never really wanted to go pro and found out it wasn't what it's cracked up to me. Yes, there's a lot more money in it these days but, for most boxers, everything they get is very hard-earned.

The amateur game was what I fell in love with after getting over my early reservations. The people I met were great, with my trainers Arthur and Harold almost becoming two more dads. Fights came thick and fast and I did very well. Leaving the Nottingham School of Boxing, my base from that first night, was the beginning of the end. That happened because I was beginning to take my eye off the ball in favour of other natural things in a young man's life. After having a couple of girlfriends, my relationship with Val became more serious. I was only 19 when we got married and moved over the border to Selston in Derbyshire, where Val had lived all her life, but too far away for me to stay at the club.

I wanted to stay in Hyson Green and at the Nottingham School of Boxing club with Arthur and Harold, but Val was having none of it. When I broke the news to Harold, he was devastated. He had trained me from a kid to near the top of the amateur game. Altogether this was a difficult time of change. Dad was slowly getting worse, Mum working like a slave and here I was; leaving home, getting married and starting all over again.

At first, I was lucky. My search for a more convenient place to box led to Saxon Amateur Boxing Club, above the Sun Inn pub, in Somercotes. It was there that, as Harold and Arthur recommended, I was taken under the wing of Ken Page, whom I already knew from my Nottingham days. The club had a good reputation with Ken, a former professional, being well respected in the sport. He soon took to me and wanted me in what he called his "top shop" of fighters.

Ken was a great trainer at amateur level. Harold had rung him to explain who and what I was. He had a lot of time for Harold and they had known each other for God knows how long. I went along to the Saxon club where he and assistant Frank Jones put me through my paces. I did speedball work and a little light sparring, so they could take a look at me. At the end, Ken called me over, said he was impressed and that he had a few fights for me.

But, for very good reasons, my fights began to dry up. My success in the ring over the years started to count against me. Matchmakers looked at my fight card to check my amateur record and didn't want their boxers in the ring with me. They were looking for suitable matches in terms of age and experience and I had outgrown them.

Ken brought the issue home to me when he asked how many of my last 15 potential fights had actually taken place. The answer was only two! I had run out of opponents. Even so, my turning pro came about because of circumstances in Ken's life. He had taken us as a group to fight in Guernsey after getting verbal permission from the Amateur Boxing Association. We had a good time, winning eight out of the 10 fights, yet there was hell to play for Ken when we got back home. He was harshly banned by the ABA when they pointed out he hadn't given written approval. So, he faced being forced out of the sport after 30-odd years. The only way he could stay in boxing, which was his life, was to turn pro. And he could no longer look after me unless I did the same.

That forced my hand, even though my heart wasn't fully in it. I thought about packing in boxing myself, telling Ken

I needed time to think about my future. The idea of going into something I knew very little about didn't appeal to me. The only reason I said yes to Ken was that otherwise, all my training and the endless hours Dad had given to me would have gone by the board.

With the decision made, I felt better. I was still a young man and the idea of television and newspapers, winning titles and making big money was exciting. Yet, speaking with boxers who had tasted the professional life, I began to fear I had made a big mistake. They warned me of managers ripping boxers off, and that this wasn't the gentleman's sport I was used to. It turned out that they were so right!

I liked Ken as a person and have nothing against him. He was a good man, but I'm not sure Harold and Arthur knew him quite as well as they thought. I saw him daily and, in that sense, he was a proper manager But, in many ways, he was as lost in the professional world as I was. As an amateur, he knew the game and the people and was able to dominate and get most things done on his own terms.

But his 'my way or no way' attitude didn't cut it at the higher level and he wasn't willing to learn. He was taken to one side and told harsh truths, but shrugged off such advice. I found myself making a few enemies because my manager had a reputation for being a handful.

We agreed Ken would take 25 per cent of my earnings as manager. He also wanted more for taking the role of trainer, but I couldn't afford that from the meagre purses I was getting. The trainer's role is important, particularly in the ring. It was good I was able to trust Ken's advice, but I had no option. Otherwise, we had to settle for what they term 'house' cornermen, because we couldn't afford to employ our own.

My early experiences as a pro were mirrored throughout my career. The most important people in the sport should be the boxers. But they are usually the last to know what is going on. The communication in the professional business is mostly between managers and promoters, with boxers then being told who and when they are fighting and for how much without being consulted.

I'm not criticising my managers as people – Dave Needman apart, I got on well with all of them – but it was my experience that nobody really cares for the people who really do the business and put bums on seats. I say I was a professional. In truth, I was a semi-pro because, like many boxers, I still needed a full-time job to make up my money. I was getting purses of between £200 and £300 in the early days, rising to a maximum of between £4,000 and £5,000 later in my career.

My purse for my first professional fight was as low as £140. From that, I had to pay Ken and all my expenses. The fight was in Cambridge, so that cost petrol money there and back. I also had to take the day off from work as the fight was on a Friday night. With necessary extras, such as food and drink on the way to and from the venue, I ended up making a small loss.

Compare that with amateur boxing where I didn't get paid for fighting, yet all my outgoings were covered. The venue covered our travel, giving us a food ticket for sandwiches and crisps. If we were travelling a fair distance, the organisers paid for an overnight stay. All this and we picked up trophies and prizes for winning.

I knew from day one turning professional was a risk when I had so much on my plate. I became a professional in 1977 after getting married to Val in 1975 and the birth of our first daughter Tara the following year. That meant there was a lot at stake for me. I was pleased to win my first fight, a comfortable points success over Peter Snowsel from Cambridge. Dad was as happy as Larry, although he couldn't be there because of his health.

Despite being in a very bad way with the cancer, Dad's stubborn ways meant he stuck to his own ideas how to ease his pain. He discovered an ointment which he thought could cure anything – even cancer. This was a live soot from the coal fire which he mixed with gelatin into what looked like a black jelly. It wasn't enough to take this through his mouth; Dad thought he needed to get it directly into his bloodstream by cutting himself and inserting the jelly twice daily. It was horrible to watch, and drove both Mum and I mad. But he wouldn't be told.

When Dad was taken into Nottingham General Hospital, I visited him a few times, but it wasn't easy for me. I didn't have a reliable vehicle and relied on the bus, meaning there wasn't much time left to see him. I was working for Kaymar Industrial Furniture at Pinxton and loved my job. I was fetching my sandwiches from my car one morning when Dave Palmer, one of the managers, put his hand on my shoulder and said he had something to tell me. He didn't need to say a word – I knew.

Dad had passed away.

I went home as quickly as I could. Mum and I were both in pieces. That was when I really could have done with having a brother or a sister. There was so much running around to do when I wasn't in a good frame of mind. It felt like my whole world had just collapsed and I lost my will to live for a while.

Dad was my hero and I honestly don't know how I got

through that horrible time. We had our fall-outs like any father and son, but he was always there for me and Mum. He never had a great deal to give us materially but, what he had, he shared. My boxing suffered afterwards but I knew I couldn't give it up. Dad wouldn't have wanted me to. Continuing to fight, although my heart wasn't in it, was one way I could hold on to him.

I'll be honest and say that at that time, I couldn't give a shit. I'm not sure I even went into a gym between my first and second fights. I couldn't be bothered and it was no surprise I was well beaten on points. I had three professional fights under Ken's management – the last one being in March 1978.

By this time I had a new job at Plyglass at Somercotes, having been set on though Frank Jones. I worked regular days and it was a five-mile bike ride from home. All went well at first as my work was only half a mile from training. I rounded off a long day riding up the long hill into Selston. But Frank telling the gaffer about my sporting career proved a mistake. He was worried about me taking time off and this affected the way he treated me. Soon afterwards he took me off days and put me on afternoons and nights, making it more difficult for me to train.

I got the impression he was green-eyed. He had been a footballer who hadn't made the grade, and was perhaps jealous of me being a professional boxer. I never asked to be treated any differently because of my boxing but the gaffer's comments got to me. So much so I wrote my resignation letter, put my coat on and went into his office.

He was narky, saying I had no right to walk in without his permission and making nasty comments to me. That's when I lost it. I hit him and he fell to the ground. I told him never to speak to me like that again and, luckily, didn't hear any more about the incident. I apologised to Frank because I felt I'd let him down. He told me the gaffer was still walking around with a black chin. That's because I didn't hit him with my full power.

Val backed me in some practical ways, such as washing my kit, but was never 100 per cent behind my boxing. It was the same with my daughters, who were neither for nor against it. My wife did have a point, though. She told me I was losing fights I should be winning and that, if I was going to box, I needed to do it properly. If not, better to pack it in before I got hurt.

I trained harder for a while but couldn't sustain it without Dad to push me. He would ask me why I had stopped after I had done 100 press ups and without him, I was never fully motivated. I bumped into Dave Needham again after I split with Ken Page. When I said I was on my own, he invited me to come and train with him and said he would get me fights. He had a few boxers with him, including Dennis Sheehan and Alan Pearson. We didn't sign a contract or anything like that but we worked together for about a year.

Dave was a very successful boxer, winning a Commonwealth Games gold medal in the 1970s and British bantamweight and featherweight titles. When I began boxing, Dad wanted me to be like Dave Needham, but my experience with him would have burst his bubble. It was a very good thing Dad wasn't around to find out about the Dave Needham I got to know. He would have been horrified.

Dave was good at coming across as your friend. But he never fully had my trust and certainly didn't do anything to earn it. Before writing this, I got permission from Dave's brother, so don't think I am having a go at the dead because he can no longer fight back. Putting it in a nutshell, if you were a woman or a bottle of lager, Dave was interested in you. He used boxers to get what he wanted.

Moving from Ken Page's management to Dave Needham did have one immediate benefit – going back to the Nottingham School of Boxing. It was a strange feeling, walking through the same garage door where my boxing had begun 13 years ago. Immediately it took me back to the first day I had gone there with Dad and he had nearly stumbled in the dim light. Exploring further, it was as if nothing had changed.

Same old changing room with horsehair boxing gloves hanging on the wall, the old Avery sliding scales, the seat to put my kit on and old gas fire. The gym was unchanged too, with its ground level boxing ring and skipping ropes on the wall. It felt good, to be honest. Almost like going home.

I was always the outsider in Needham's camp. He was very good mates with Sheehan and used Pearson as his chauffeur. As an amateur, I had knocked about with Sheehan's older brother Mick. whilst he and Sheehan were buddies. This was one reason I never hit it off with Dennis as well, as he was big friends with Needham. The best I can say is that we coped with each other.

I didn't take long to realise Needham's methods didn't suit me. We trained very hard, but he insisted on taking us out drinking afterwards. My three-wheeler was used as a taxi to take us to Mortimer's Cavern, near Trent Polytechnic in Nottingham. It was a very busy pub and Dave was at home there. As soon as we got inside, he ordered five bottles of lager and asked for 12 more to be put on ice. He started drinking very quickly and after a second bottle soon followed, I was beginning to worry. I was driving home and didn't want to risk it. A couple of bottles of lager was enough to knock me out, as I wasn't a big drinker.

Unknown to Needham, I often offered my second bottle to anyone within sight to avoid drinking it. He was too consumed with his own drink and women to notice. Maybe I was taking things too seriously, I don't know. But, for me, there's more to life than drinking. By now I had two kids at home and responsibilities. I didn't need this kind of aggro.

I also realised Needham was more interested in Sheehan. Needham spoke quite openly. The two of us sparred together and he said I wasn't good or quick enough to beat him. I don't think he rated me and thought he wasn't going to make the same money from me as he did with Sheehan. Needham also used me to cover up his womanising. He was terrible, to be honest. Several times he asked me to confirm his cover story to his wife, Mandy, when he thought he was on to a 'certainty'. Mandy trusted me and I hated doing it. I was there as a professional boxer; I didn't want anything to do with his lifestyle.

I would describe Needham more as a go-between than a manager. He arranged fights for me, but didn't give guidance or direction. Sometimes he didn't even attend my fights. At one show, where I had been abandoned, I bumped into Tony Sibson's manager Carl Gunns in the dressing room. "How are things going with Dave Needham?" he asked. The grin and knowing look on his face said more than his question. "To be honest with you, I'm not very happy," I replied. "If you ever want to change, give me a ring," he said, passing me his telephone number.

When I had the privilege of fighting at the Royal Albert Hall in London, I discovered Needham was also ripping me off financially. The way we worked things was that Needham told me my purse for each fight, then collected the money himself. I understood his cut was included, then he handed the rest to me. It started off as a good night. I'd never even been to the Royal Albert Hall before, even as a spectator, and was up for the fight against Sid Smith, a Londoner and a highly-respected fighter.

Despite Sid's good record, I gave him such a good eight-round fight he admitted afterwards he had lost, despite getting the points decision.

Needham had been in my corner during the fight but when I walked back to the dressing room, he had vanished. Knowing Needham's social habits, I had no idea if he was coming back. The fight was arranged through Needham's partnership with well-known promoter Mickey Duff, but there was no way of grabbing a word with him as he was always busy on show night.

I spoke with one of the ringside officials about collecting my money. He had a good laugh about helping to take my gloves off, then handed me the envelope. It contained about three times as much as I expected. Had I made a mistake? Back in the dressing room, I dug out my wallet and, sure enough, I had remembered correctly.

This was a novelty for the Boxing Board of Control official. Boxers didn't normally complain about being overpaid! I asked him to check if they had made an error, but he said the money was right. Now there was no doubt in my mind – Needham had arranged most of the purse for himself. My first worry was how to get home. We had stayed at Mandy's parents' house in London, but at least I had the cash to travel home, if necessary.

As I was walking out of the Albert Hall, Needham came back in. It was about two hours after the fight and I presumed he had been out with a woman. He was keen to go clubbing rather than back to the house, but I told him I wasn't interested. I didn't want him driving me back up the motorway next day the worse for wear.

We stayed the night at the house and, during the journey next day, he finally asked me if I had picked up the money. I said yes and asked him how much he was expecting. Back at his house in Wollaton, where I had parked my car, I said I wasn't going to give him his money. This would make up for the times he had ripped me off in the past. He wasn't happy and slammed the door behind him.

My happy memories of the Nottingham School of Boxing with Dad were now being overtaken by awkward times with Needham. But a few days later, he phoned me out of the blue as if nothing had happened. Sheehan and Pearson were at training and, at the end of the night, he expected me to take the three of them in my three-wheeler to Mortimer's Cavern. I said I couldn't fit them all in and went home.

There was one more social invitation. Needham said they were going out at the weekend to The White Hart at Arnold and our partners were invited. I probably wouldn't have come otherwise, and Val agreed to come with me. When we arrived at the pub, there were five or six lads, but no wives.

As usual, Needham was eyeing up a woman – in this case, the new barmaid. He wanted us to talk to her and press his case for a date. I felt so sorry for his wife, who was very pretty and a lovely person. It was no surprise to me when I found later that they had divorced.

I could see Val was distressed. She told me Needham had tried it on with her by grabbing her arse and making comments. So I bided my time, waited until Needham went to the toilet and followed him in. He was full of small talk about what a good night it was. He washed his hands and zipped up before I said 'look up' and I caught him with a right hand, followed by a few lefts.

Needham buckled and fell to the floor. He was bleeding heavily. I left him there and told Val we were going. I knew his henchmen would have been on my case. I saw Needham at a show afterwards. He scowled at me as I said: "In case, you haven't realised, we're finished."

There was a gap after cutting ties with Needham when I ticked over without training particularly hard, before ringing Carl Gunns. We met up – eventually, after I had struggled to find his house – and I told him more about my problems with Needham. He agreed to take me on and get me fights, and did just that. Carl was a good man who arranged a lot of bouts for me, but he didn't turn up for 90 per cent of them.

One example was when he booked me to fight Damien Fryers at Belfast's King's Hall in March 1983. I asked what the travel arrangements were for both of us and he made it clear he wasn't going. It was the first time I had been on an aeroplane in my life and it wasn't nice. There was a big storm on the flight to Ireland, which caused the small plane to drop very suddenly. A stewardess said it was the worst storm for a long time.

In Belfast, the fight organisers weren't happy. Not only was Carl Gunns not coming, I had no cornermen with me either. I told them not to shoot the messenger, but they were clearly angry about having to make last-minute arrangements to ensure the fight went on. Worse followed on the scales. I was seven pounds over the agreed weight as

Gunns had given me the wrong information. Told the fight was off, I stood my ground. I knew I could weigh in again four hours later.

I went back to the hotel and asked for the sauna to be turned up to the maximum temperature. I piled on as many layers of clothing as I could, including tracksuit, bin-liner and a woolly hat, to keep the heat in. I got out the skipping rope and went full pelt. I also asked staff to keep an eye on me as I knew I was likely to pass out – which I did, two or three times. After one of the most frantic sessions of my life, I climbed back onto the scales with a couple of minutes to spare and had lost nine and a half pounds in four hours. All of it in water.

It was always going to be hard work against Damien, a local lad in front of his home crowd. But when I got into the ring and saw three of him, the night had got a lot tougher. His first jab made my eyes go fuzzy. Somehow, I continued and did so well Damien told me in the dressing room I had won. But the judges' decision went with the home fighter. I was disappointed, but that was nothing compared with what was to come.

The Europa Hotel was known as the most bombed hotel in the world, having been attacked 36 times during The Troubles in Northern Ireland, and I was dropping off to sleep in my top floor room when I heard a terrific bang. I shot out of bed, looked out the window and there was glass and debris everywhere. That was enough. I gathered my belongings as quickly as I could and ran like lightning down the stairs, not trusting the lift. I told the receptionist I was off and asked for a number for a cab. It was hours before my plane, but I felt safer at the airport.

Then we had a repeat of the first storm on the way back

– only worse! I felt anything but safe in a very small pro-
peller plane being thrown about. White-faced and genuinely scared, I felt like kissing the ground with relief when
we landed. When I told Carl the story of my fight and the
problems I had gone through, he shrugged off his absence
in a matter-of-fact way.

A couple of days after returning home, I started to feel
sick and dizzy. I was suffering from acute dehydration and
got a lecture from my GP. My actions had put my kidneys
at risk. He gave me tablets and told me to drink as much
water as I could. It was about four to six weeks before I was
back to full health.

Carl's priority was always Tony Sibson, who became
Commonwealth and European champion and fought the
great Marvin Hagler for the world middleweight crown. I
sparred with Sibbo a couple of times without really getting
to know him, at a time when he was making waves with 24
wins and a draw from his first 25 professional fights.

Tony was first on a bill where I was fighting and I asked
Carl who he was fighting. Gunns said his opponent hadn't
had many fights. I pressed him twice more for a name before he told me it was Lotty Mwale, from Zambia.

"Have you done your homework on him?" I asked. I took
a keen interest in amateur boxing and knew Mwale was
outstanding. He fought about 300 times without being
beaten. I saw from Gunns' reaction that he had no idea. Opponents are chosen very carefully, particularly for a boxer
being groomed for a world title shot. There's no way they
would have allowed him to get in the ring with Mwale had
they studied his record.

I looked through the curtain as Mwale landed an almighty punch in the first round that sentenced Sibbo to his

first professional defeat. I asked Carl what the result was when I saw him before my fight. Boxing should be about two fighters getting in the ring and doing the business. Everyone interested in the sport knows it, but managers too often exploit the public and ruin their entertainment. To be honest, their main aim is to fill their own pockets rather than benefit their fighter and the fans.

I never formally finished with Carl Gunns. We just fizzled out. He phoned me to say a boxer had pulled out and I had a fight that night and I refused. That happened two, three, maybe four times, before he stopped calling me and I lost contact with him. Instead, I joined up with Jimmy Gill, from Nottingham, who became my fourth and last manager as a pro. Jimmy was someone I had read about and based at a boxing gym off Mansfield Road. When I went to see him, he was very keen on working with me.

Jimmy is a nice guy but had one major problem – alcohol. My mate Steve Holbrook had already picked up on this when Jimmy rang at 2.30pm to tell me about a fight that evening in Liverpool. I accepted the gig and there was no time to waste. Knowing Jimmy, Steve suggested we would be safer going down in his small Fiesta than the manager's six-litre Mercedes. Jimmy, though, was adamant we went in his car as another boxer, Willie Wilson, was coming with us.

He drove to Liverpool like a crackpot, which didn't ease our nerves. Before my fight, Jimmy came into the changing room to put my wraps on and smelt strongly of alcohol. He nearly tripped over the ropes when we went into the ring. Afterwards Jimmy said what none of us needed to hear – he wanted to go for a drink before going home. Willie and I decided to stay at the venue whilst Steve suggested the two of them go for a meal.

About half an hour later Steve walked back in. "I'm going to kill that manager of yours," he said. I asked where he was and he said he had no idea. Then he told me the story. Jimmy and Steve had been to a Chinese restaurant, with Jimmy bringing in a half bottle of whiskey. Steve ordered a regular meal whilst Jimmy went for about 20 items. When the first arrived, he plunged face first into his food.

After Steve brought him back round, Jimmy said he was off to the toilet. Steve followed as he disappeared out of the first door he came to, which slammed behind him, leaving both of them in the backyard. Four or five Chinese men then appeared carrying meat cleavers, with Steve shouting to Jimmy: "They're going to kill us." In an instant, Jimmy came round from his slumber and somehow climbed over a fence like Spiderman, in Steve's words. Steve was then left to settle the bill, which was more than £80 – a very large amount for a meal in the 1980s.

Whilst Steve was still saying what he thought of Jimmy, the man himself staggered through the door. We tried to persuade him to hand over the car keys, but he wasn't having any of it. It was his car and he was driving. As the three of us sat in the back, Willie said: "Perhaps the impact will be less here!"

Jimmy zig-zagged across the road. He complained about his suspension after driving over cat's eyes and crashed through a barrier before we spotted the inevitable blue lights behind us. I told Jimmy to pull over, but he put his foot down. After a second, bigger police car joined the chase, he eventually brought the car to a halt. What happened next will probably remain a mystery for the rest of my life.

Jimmy got out, walked towards the police car and said

very calmly: "Hello, officer, what appears to be the problem?" He also explained he used to be a police officer. The conversation continued until the police told him to be on his way. No arrest, no breath test, nothing. Jimmy continued in his unsteady way until I grabbed him by the throat and warned I'd kill him unless he stopped the car. We had a three or four-hour sleep before Jimmy, still not fully recovered, drove the rest of the way home.

There were one or two fights I wish I hadn't taken on for personal reasons. Being top of the bill at The Albany Hotel in Nottingham was great but that turned sour when my opponent pulled out a couple of days before. When Jimmy said my new opponent was Seamus Casey, I wasn't happy because I knew him too well. I trained Seamus as an amateur at South Normanton Boxing Club, teaching him how and when to throw shots. So, I had a good idea before he came into the ring every move he was going to make. That wasn't fair on either of us.

Seamus came into my dressing room before the fight, saying he had an important fight coming up and asking me not to throw anything too big. I didn't know whether he was joking but told him to get out. I stayed in the dressing room alone and went to sleep, asking Jimmy to wake me up about an hour before the fight. When we were announced and the referee ushered us into the centre of the ring, I didn't want to be there.

When the fight started, I hit him with a right uppercut and saw him stagger backwards. Normally I would have followed in for the kill, but I was gentle and took my time. The same pattern followed round by round as I gave Seamus a boxing lesson to win on points. I had no intention of hurting him.

A fight against Nick Vardy, broadcast on ITV's *World of Sport* with former world champion John Conteh doing the summarising, also left a strange feeling. Having sparred with Vardy as an amateur, I knew his style very well – he swung like a madman and could really hit, but left himself wide open. On this occasion, he was so cautious he barely left a mark on me as I won on points. Afterwards we talked and he suggested a return. There was no way that was going to happen.

Generally, I was struggling to rise to the occasion. I was never going to let anyone down – I don't do things like that – but wasn't enthralled with boxing any more. I could easily have been persuaded to give it up before I did. I had good intentions of going for a six-mile run then ended up running around the block. I was losing partly because I wasn't fit enough. Because I wasn't training 100 per cent, there were amateurs who would have beaten me. I turned up at fights with no interest in what happened. I shouldn't have been fighting in that state of mind – and that happened throughout most of my professional career.

When I started work at Underwood pit, I thought being a boxer was going to help. The manager seemed keen on the idea and even promised sponsorship. This was something I wouldn't have dreamt of asking for. He was also thoughtful in telling me there was an opening in the blacksmith's shop rather than going down the mine as this would be better for me. It would have been difficult to combine training with shift work. So again, without asking, I was working convenient hours of eight o'clock in the morning until four in the afternoon and felt at home in the shop, where I was the 'baby blacksmith'. My workmates were time-served guys in their mid-fifties and always there to help me.

I loved the first couple of months, but then came a very sudden change of heart. The manager came into the shop in a bad mood, telling me: "You, get your helmet, you're going down the pit with me!" He was picking on two or three of us. We were gobsmacked. The shop manager tried to reason with him, but he wouldn't back down.

Because I'd been taught to stand up for myself, I wasn't having it. I took my helmet off in front of the lads, who were cheering me, and told him to fuck his job, reminding him that the sponsorship had been an empty promise. I'm a man of my word. He had told me I wasn't working down the pit and then gone back on it. I left Underwood with my chin held high. I found out later why he had been so brutal with us. I bumped into the manager of the blacksmith's shop a few years later and he said the manager had just found his wife in bed with another bloke.

The sponsorship cheque had come through shortly afterwards and he had asked the shop manager whether I was likely to come back. His answer was that once someone has shit on Steve, there's no going back and from there I went back to Kaymar. The job was demanding and not as well paid as previous ones but, with the help of overtime, I enjoyed it very much and stayed for 12 or 13 years.

My retirement from professional boxing in 1986 was caused by boxing politics and my nemesis, Dave Needham. I was chasing the Midlands light middleweight title, held by Dennis Sheehan, and it didn't take a genius to work out Needham was going to make it very hard for me to get a title shot. Things came to a head after a title fight between Sheehan and Richard Wilson in Leicester hit the rocks. Wilson pulled out on the day for some reason and the promoters had a real problem. Every ticket had been sold and there weren't many suitable boxers who fancied fighting Shee-han. Jimmy Gill rang at lunchtime asking about my fitness. I knew he was fishing, so asked him to get to the point – was I able and willing to fight Sheehan over eight rounds later that day?

My answer was a definite yes. I was in very good condi-tion and Sheehan was the guy I'd been chasing. Needham wasn't in charge of the promotion but must have known about his man's new opponent. I guess he still thought I wasn't much good, and Sheehan would win easily.

Having to make my own way to Leicester made no dif-ference. I'd have run there backwards to fight Sheehan and win the title. I knew the odds and the crowd were against me but was confident in my own ability. This was my chance to take a big step forward. Trainer John Turner, who drove me to Leicester, was the only friendly face at the venue. Everyone else was supporting Sheehan. That was okay, I could handle that, but I knew something was both-ering Johnny after the weigh-in. He was evasive, at first, but I pinned him down. The title wasn't on the line after all because I wasn't the named opponent.

I knew what was happening – Needham didn't want me to get hold of his man's crown. I had every right to pull out and go back home there and then. But I told Jimmy I was still going to fight, even without the title. If I won, Needham would surely be obliged to give me a re-match for the title?

I wasn't just fighting Dennis Sheehan that night, I was fighting Dave Needham. This was my chance to prove a point. The crowd went crazy when he entered the ring. He growled at me when the referee ushered us into the centre of the ring to give us his instructions. I smirked and went back to my corner.

Sheehan came out hard in the first round. He jabbed away and I discovered why he was a champion. He edged the first three minutes. I had held back to see what Sheehan had to offer and landed more in round two. The third also went my way, but it was the fourth when things really swung in my favour. I hit him with huge hooks almost at will and the champion took a standing count of eight.

This was my chance. I started the fifth quickly and cut him. It was bad, from the corner of his eye to his nose. He was in no condition to fight back and the referee jumped in and stopped the fight. I had won. First thing I did afterwards was remind Needham exactly what I thought about him.

Even then, I never got my title fight. I had a few bouts after that, but the one I really wanted never came about. Jimmy offered a financial package and I added £1,000 on top from my own pocket. But nothing we put forward was acceptable. I knew enough about the business to know I was hitting my head against a brick wall.

That was it. I called time on my boxing career at the age of 32. I still loved the sport, but hated the politics and I'd had more than enough. My last fight was down south somewhere – I don't remember much about it. I entertained crowds and gave it my all whenever I was in the ring. But I was a million miles short of winning a major title.

4

LOVE AND STITCHES ON THE DOORS

By Lucy Ward

I met Steve when, after the end of a 10-year relationship, I started going out in Mansfield on a Friday and Saturday night with my friend Kim. Steve was a doorman at The Banque pub and when we got to the door, Kim flung her arms round Steve. I was more reserved, which is my nature. He was always polite to me and one day my sister told me, as we were leaving The Banque, that she thought Steve liked me.

I didn't take a lot of notice, for two reasons – doormen have a bad reputation, and Steve was older than me. But I soon found out he was no typical doorman. He was a gentleman with a heart of gold and certainly no thug. Steve saw me in a nice skirt and top one evening and asked: "How does your boyfriend let you out looking like that?"

I told him I had no boyfriend – we had split up in July and I wasn't going back. Steve asked if I'd like to go out one night and I said: "Yes, why not?" He asked for my telephone number and I blurted it out. Then I saw him go to the bar, ask for a piece of paper and write it down. He did well to remember it!

About two weeks later, Kim and I saw him coming out of The Swan public house in Mansfield, then at the nightclub. Steve was with friends, but we had a little chat. I was impressed because he pronounced my name right – my full name is Louisa – and then he

gave me a kiss on the cheek. It was October 30, 2001, when we first
went out. He picked me up from Kim's house and was a little ner-
vous as he clipped the kerb twice driving along Nottingham Road
on the way to The Commodore, where we had a meal.
Soon we were going out almost every night – Smiley Sam's and the
cinema were two of my favourites. By this time, the age gap didn't
matter at all – we were going with the flow.
It was a long time before I found out Steve was a boxer and it
happened by accident. Someone came up to him and said: "Hey,
champ, are you still fighting?" I was impressed. There was a lot I
still didn't know about this man...

Boxing can be a very dangerous sport, but I'll let you into a little secret. I have had more than 300 stitches in my life and only three of those were the result of professional boxing. Much of the rest and a whole host of adventures and close scrapes have come from working on the doors.

In some ways, boxing and security work go together. They include some of the same skills, handling very difficult situations and getting the job done with as little harm to life and limb as possible. Like my boxing, the door work had its roots from very early in my life. I tell folk I never chose to be a doorman; it chose me! It all started when I went to school discos at Ellis Guilford.

Whilst others danced, I watched – and a teacher commented on it. I told him dancing wasn't really my thing, but I enjoyed listening to the music. The other reason I stood just in front of the wall, during a time when I was being bullied at school, was to avoid problems caused by idiots. Standing there, I had the perfect vantage point to see in all directions with no chance of anyone creeping up behind me. "You're a proper little doorman, aren't you?" the teacher said.

"Doorman?" I replied. "I suppose so..." And my story goes from there. Afterwards a couple of staff, music teacher Mr. Humperdinck – yes, honestly! – and Mr. Clarke, approached me two or three times during a school disco to ask if I'd seen anything. I didn't want to tell on others, but I had spotted lads smoking and boys and girls going near the bike sheds for what comes naturally. There I was, at the age of 14, acting like a doorman!

I was 18 when I really started working in security and I was on the doors or doing close protection work for about 30 years, both during my professional boxing career and beyond. My first place, if I remember correctly, was Matlock Pavilion, where I worked Friday and Saturday nights for about a year. It was a heavy rock pub which attracted a lot of bikers and young farmers, who tended to be buggers – and big ones at that.

I got to know some of the ropes early on; others came from experience. It isn't the doorman's job to try to make a name for himself. The ideal night is when security staff slip into the background without being noticed. Venue owners want everyone to have a nice night with no trouble, and there were plenty of evenings like that. It was never my scene to dress in a dicky bow and black suit. I preferred to wear something more comfortable. Once I had been at one place for a while it didn't matter anyway because everyone knew I was a doorman.

The secret of being an effective doorman is to be diplomatic – firm but fair. Once I made my mind up, I said my piece and stuck with it. It wasn't my job to explain why I didn't let someone in and, if you back down even once, word gets round and that leads to more problems. Here's the first rule of the game: it's much easier not to let a troublemaker in, than drag them out. I spoke with them politely, telling them there were plenty of other places they could try, but they weren't coming in here.

I soon started passing on tips to others. I worked with a young guy about six foot six, 17 stone and looking to make a name for himself. I could see he waded straight in as soon as he saw any trouble, so I dragged him back. "You go in there now and who have you got to look out for most?" I asked. "The one who is waiting for you!" Often, it's not the people fighting who cause most grief, but someone on the edge of it all who takes you by surprise. I was always on the lookout for someone with a bottle.

The first move is to take a good look at what is going on. In a venue with two or more floors, it's worth taking an aerial view. Then when you go into the room, don't run. That causes more disturbance and people panic. I walked in briskly but could still look in the mirrors and see everything and everyone around me. That way I could better size up what was likely to happen next. Taking extra time also allows those involved in the fight to punch themselves out and become tired. That way they are going to be easier to move.

I challenged myself to be a good doorman; better than the rest. It's important how you speak with customers. Taking time to talk with them politely and showing you remember them pays dividends. I'd tell a woman regular I liked the way she had done her hair, or ask if those were new shoes. They soon got to know me and that can be very helpful.

Not many customers in those early days knew I was a boxer. I didn't want to wear that as a badge in case it made me a target. I'll give you an example from when I was about 40 years old. A young lad, who knew I was a boxer, approached the door with a few young women in the background. Perhaps trying to impress them, he started goading me.

"I reckon I can do you!" he said. I must have heard those words a thousand times before. "Well, you're just going to have to 'reckon' because you're never going to find out," I replied. Of course, I didn't want to fight and hoped he'd move on. But this young man was particularly stubborn and wouldn't take no for an answer. Eventually I got to the point where, to keep my self-respect, I had to do something.

I asked why he wanted to hurt someone of 40 – he must have been in his early to mid-twenties. But he wouldn't let it go. I presumed he wanted to look tough. He shaped up to box me, so I took him by surprise by turning to martial arts. Apart from my boxing, I had trained in two forms of kung fu and it didn't take me long to land a telling blow that put him flat out on the floor. "Doesn't he look stupid?" I said as he lay in a pool of blood before I dragged him from the doorway. I didn't want him to ruin anyone else's night.

He was one man who did come back to say sorry. "I would like to apologise for the way I treated you," he said. "Go away!" I answered. "I don't want your sort in this place." You might think I was being harsh, but I'd told him he was banned and I wasn't going back on it. I'd seen the way he'd kicked off with me without any provocation and thought he could do the same thing again.

Mostly, I worked in Nottingham and Mansfield but also did shifts in cities such as London and Sheffield. I worked at the Corn Exchange in Nottingham, round the corner from Rosie O'Brien's. I was the head doorman, so I could choose my staff and knew my back was well covered. Through working there, I made lifelong buddies in Rob Marshall and Andy Fox. Between us we found ourselves in some very sticky situations but always came out on top.

I worked with some great lads there and had great fun with the punters. They got to know us and there was no real trouble. There was always the odd drunk or someone who thought he could fight the world, but mainly it was a good pub and was run very well.

We would always be up for a joke, too, with a £20 note, a fishing line and a packed pub on a Friday night. We put the note on the floor and watched for the sucker thinking this was their lucky night. Sure as chocolate melts, a drunk would spot the note and try to pick it up. We tugged it and this half-pissed idiot chased it all over the place. Then they clicked on and the place was in uproar. It was a good time to be on the doors in many ways.

I worked with a great, young lad I will call Dave. He was a good friend and so was his wife. He was big into judo; there was even talk of him making the national team for the Commonwealth Games. The manager told me to take him under my wing and keep an eye on him. On his first night working with us, trouble kicked off and Dave launched himself straight into the middle of it, no holding back.

A couple of weeks went by and Dave invited me back to his house to have a meal. It was there I got to know his wife and his little boy. It was nice to see a young man with a head on his shoulders and a young family. At the time I envied him a little for that. A couple of more weeks went by and a girl started coming to the pub – a real stunner, with legs up to her armpits and long brown hair. Beautiful.

It was clear she fancied Dave and they started to flirt. I warned him not to let it go beyond that or he might lose what he really treasured. The old saying "a prick bigger than the brain" springs to mind because he was at it with her within weeks. He would ring his wife and tell her he was going to some other pub or club after his shift and be late home. Then he went to her place and rolled home about six in the morning.

I told him I thought too much of his wife to lie for him and it went on for months, maybe a year or so. Then the Corn Exchange manager rang me at the concrete factory where I worked, telling me the police needed to see me. He didn't give me any details but hinted it was serious and I was racking my brain, wondering whether it was some drunk I'd hit too hard.

About 9pm, two coppers arrived at my door. They were in plain clothes, so I knew they weren't mucking about. "Have you seen this young woman?" they asked, showing me a mug shot of Dave's fancy piece. I told them her name. One of the coppers smiled and told me her real name.

Then came the bombshell. She was one of the city's biggest cocaine dealers and was using Dave to get her stuff into the pub, along with another half-a-dozen pubs and clubs in the city. Dave was in on it. What a shock! I told them my mate wouldn't do any such thing when out came the photographs and a video. Sure enough, there he was with bags of white powder in his hand at the back of the pub and outside another club. They said he was earning five or six grand a week.

Dave and his fancy woman got nicked, and his life was

over. He lost it all – job, wife, kid and his freedom. He got five years in jail, she got three – all down to thinking you can do anything as a doorman and everyone fears or loves you.

Eventually the landlord moved to Mansfield and needed someone with a clean bill of criminal health to take charge of a team of doormen. That's how I came to work at The Banque, the former NatWest Bank in Mansfield. It was a two-level pub where I recruited and worked with about half-a-dozen staff. I always positioned myself on the front door to stop potential trouble at source.

One night a group of 15 Hull City supporters came to the door of the very lively and popular pub. It was after a football match against Mansfield Town and, as I knew there were many Stags fans inside, there was no way they were coming in. They were cocky and not going to accept no for an answer. One asked: "What are you going to do to stop us?"

I was diplomatic, but made it very clear I wasn't going to change my mind. Eventually they thought better of it and turned around and walked away as I gave a huge sigh of relief. No way could I have handled all 15 of them! Then I turned around and saw about 50 people near the entrance sticking up for me. That all came about because of the relationships I'd built up with them.

One night a woman caught my attention. She called me by name and said she'd always reckoned I was a fair guy but there was something she wanted to tell me about. She took me by the hand and led me into the middle of the pub where I saw a young guy, aged about 18 or 19, bonking hell for leather with a young woman I had let in after she produced her birth certificate.

The young man took no notice when I shouted him to

stop, so I lifted him off the woman with his you-know-what flapping all over the place. From there, I carried him to the exit, threw him out and told him he was barred – for good. When I returned to the girl, she actually asked me to finish her off, so she got the same treatment. I walked her to the door and told her she was banned for life as well. There's a time and a place for everything, and that sort of behaviour wasn't on.

There was a balcony at The Banque and a man who was having a downer was threatening to jump. He said he was going to kill himself. I told him there was no way he was going to kill himself but, landing on the carpet, he may well break his leg. I tried to talk him down, but he didn't want me near him. Life was a bitch, he said, and he didn't want any more of it.

He said he was going to aim to land on the bar to do himself more damage. He was talking rubbish because an Olympic athlete wouldn't have managed that. After a few minutes, I was losing patience. I had politely asked him a couple of times to come down. Last orders had been called and the place would be closing in five minutes – how long did he intend to keep this going for?

Those five minutes meant it was now my private time. I told him to get downstairs now. I could tolerate him mucking about in my working hours but not in my time, so I shouldered him off the balcony. He was bruised, but didn't break anything. If I hadn't done that, he may still have been there an hour later when I had curry and chips waiting for me at the chip shop for my walk back home.

Another time at The Banque, I was alerted to trouble in the toilets. I went upstairs as fast as I could and there was nobody there. I checked all the cubicles. Nothing. Suddenly my eyes were stinging. I realised straightaway that some idiot had set off CS tear gas. Next on the scene were doormen who could see my distress. I needed to go to hospital to get my eyes flushed and then went home. My eyes were still irritable the next day, but I was more concerned with finding those responsible.

The message was loud and clear. It was the Carrot Crew, a group of troublemakers who followed Mansfield Town. I called the doormen together and told them this lot were going to get a visit. If they were going to play these games, they had picked on the wrong man. What's more, I had an army of tasty lads I could call upon to help. I got them together and we went to see the big bullies – four of five of them – to give them a wake-up call. They never visited the venue again in my time, although I have to say the leader of the group is now a proper gent.

One night, after pushing a bloke who was causing trouble through the door, it became obvious that the situation could escalate. A group of 30 people congregated outside and I was concerned they wanted to get into the bar and smash it to bits. I closed the front door, telling customers to leave by the side door only. The manager wasn't happy, thinking it was costing him trade. But the alternative might well have been much worse.

I also radioed staff at the nearby Swan and between us, we had eight strong men against 30. I didn't want the police involved but thought we could deal with them, if necessary. Eventually the group got fed up with waiting to get in and dispersed without us having to do anymore.

The Swan was another venue where I had a few adventures. One night a guy had a score to settle with someone inside the pub. I could see he was going to be a problem, so told him he wasn't coming in. He had different ideas and stood in front of me, trying to push his way past with his chest sticking out. Silly boy! I didn't want to fight him and warned him he would come off second best. In the end, as he wouldn't back down or vacate the doorway, I had to forcibly remove him.

He swung for me; I just touched him to the side of the head with a blow known as "hammer fist". Catch them to the temple and it puts them off balance. When he eventually staggered away, I told one of the staff to follow him. I wasn't interested if he was planning revenge or anything like that – I was worried about him. I could see he was in a state and concerned he might collapse in the street. My intention is not to hurt people. Eventually I got a reassurance that he seemed okay.

The aim always is to stop trouble before it starts. I wasn't loud and brash on the doors. I was the quiet one. I treated people with diplomacy and respect. Sometimes I had to be strong with the landlords or owners, for their own good. Understandably their main aim is to get people through the doors and make money.

As the years went by, it became harder to relate to the youngsters. When I was 18, I was on the same level and had no problem. The next life stage is probably 30 when I was still young enough to be in touch with most of them but couldn't keep up with the younger ones. By the time I was 40, I had knowledge you can't buy. But more folk knew about my boxing and wanted to challenge me.

Changing times meant I was looking not only for knuckle dusters, but knives and even guns. The worst injury I suffered on the doors came from a machete. It was a man in a denim jacket, and I sensed trouble from the moment

I saw him. As I scanned him for weapons and put my arm up, he stabbed me with his knife. I needed 25 stitches in my left arm.

But even that wasn't the worst thing that happened to me in those days. One incident away from the doors was probably the most dangerous of the lot. It happened not far from the Cinderhill Island in Nottingham in 1993. It was about 11 o'clock at night and I was driving my car after being out running. I heard a rattle coming from the back of the vehicle, so I pulled in to see what was happening. It was probably something to do with the boot.

A few moments later another car parked directly in front. A voice from the car said: "Can you help? I'm looking for Watnall…" I knew the area like the back of my hand and walked over to the driver's side, where the smell of drugs nearly knocked me backwards. Looking in the driver's window, I saw about six people in the car, all Rastafarians, including two in the front passenger seat.

I told the driver the directions to Watnall, but he said he didn't understand. Then one of the passengers got out from the back of the car, carrying a map. As he pushed it towards me, I felt what I thought was a punch to the stomach. I reacted instantly and caught him perfectly with a leopard punch which would have broken his jaw. My next thought was to run and I made my way up some steps to a nearby house where I knocked on the door. From this vantage point, I thought I could probably take all six of them if they came for me but instead, I heard the screeching of the car driving away.

A man answered the door and I explained I'd just been involved in a fight and could I come inside. He then saw I was bleeding quite badly and it became obvious that I hadn't been punched – I had been stabbed. Police were there in a matter of minutes and I was taken by ambulance to Queen's Medical Centre for treatment. I ended up having 30 odd stitches, both inside and outside my stomach. It was the early hours of the morning and I told them to hurry up because I had to be at work at Pentos Office Furniture in Ripley at 5am.

Eventually I couldn't wait any longer, so I discharged myself and got a taxi back to my car. Luckily, it was still parked in the same spot and intact, so I got in and drove to work. By the time I got there it was 5.45am and I was 45 minutes late. The boss was straight on my case.

Still in pain, I was beginning to tell him what had happened when he stopped me and said I must have overslept. I didn't think I was going to benefit from arguing, so agreed with him and sat down to start work very gingerly.

Suddenly the news came on the radio: "Muggers sent reeling by professional boxer" and the office went deadly silent. They knew straightaway the story was about me. Now they realised I was telling the truth, but I told them to leave me alone as I didn't want to talk about it. I was still processing what had just happened.

Police came to the office to have a word with me and then took me to the station to look at a few photographs. I told one of them the guy I'd clashed with shouldn't be too difficult to identify because he had a broken jaw. "I know what happened was terrible and I understand why you did it – but he could press charges against you," one of the officers said. I thought to myself how unfair the law can be, but it never came to that. Unfortunately, the Rastafarians were never found either.

Being a doorman, I had plenty of flirty attention from

women. It's part of the territory. Attractive young ladies, dressed for the kill, almost threw themselves at me, but I didn't want to know. I even got asked if I was gay, but had no problem putting people right on that score. Apart from door work, I also did close protection work on and off. The problem wasn't the work itself but the frequent need to cover up for people. The classic situation is working with a man getting himself involved with other women, which could then lead to questions coming my way. After a while I'd had enough of it.

It worked the other way round too. A very wealthy woman I worked for, who had a crazy, jealous husband, was getting a little overfriendly with fellow guests at the casino. When I warned her that her behaviour could cause problems, she said I was paid to look after her – and that was all. When asked if she had been talking to men, I was forced, for a quieter life, to lie through my teeth, which I didn't like to do.

I like to walk down the road with my head held high without having to look over my shoulder. I didn't want this sort of aggravation. In another situation, a son was passing on all kinds of information to his mum about his dad, whom I was working for. So again, I was being asked questions I didn't want to answer. One night it came to a head, so I told the man I didn't think he was in any danger, but he needed to find a replacement for me. I explained that I couldn't take any more.

Working in those circumstances was a mug's game. You are working with extremely wealthy people and, if there's a suggestion of them splitting up, the shit well and truly hits the fan. I didn't want to be involved. People think all door-men know so many people and have friends coming out of their ears. But the truth is only a few. You have to be polite and make many contacts, but friends are rare. You never let people get too close. If you do that, lines get blurred and, if they piss about, you have to act.

Then your so-called friend becomes a pain in the arse. The old "we are mates and you can't throw me out" routine can become a big problem.

The same goes for women. A good doorman doesn't usually let a female get too close. It's a dangerous distraction and one that has cost many good doormen their jobs – and their families. There was one woman, however, whom I met on the doors and changed my life completely.

Lucy's friend threw her arms around me at the door, but it was the more reserved and polite woman who interested me more. She stood behind Kim more modestly. I think my first ever words to her were: "Are you alright, gal?"

I was working with Greg and I could see he was looking at Lucy. "Oi, back door," I told him. I wanted her treating with more respect – plus, of course, I liked the look of her myself! That was how things were – the odd word here and there when I greeted Lucy and her friend at the door – until one Saturday night, when I gave myself a rare night off. I was out on the town in Mansfield with five or six mates when my eyes fixed on Lucy in a red glittery dress fit for Kylie Minogue.

She has told the story of how we got to know each other and, yes, I was nervous that first date. I've been in the ring with people 20 or 30 years my junior who looked like King Kong without getting nervous. That's my nature. And I don't normally hit kerbs. I'm a good driver. But I knew this was important.

I didn't tell Lucy I was a boxer. I'm not a boaster. I don't go up to people and tell them: "I'm Steve Ward, I've done this and that." That's not me. I know a lot of people in the Mansfield area and they talk to me about boxing. That's how my 'secret' came out after I'd been going out with Lucy for about two years. We became engaged around that time, although I still needed to sort my divorce. I don't think either of us had any idea back then how our life together was going to develop.

5

ALTERNATIVE FIGHTING

Walking back to the changing room after my final professional fight, I was grabbed by a guy in the crowd who told me he had enjoyed my boxing career and forced something into my glove. "Take care, see you later!" he said. When I was on my own, I took off my gloves, opened the package and a roll of money fell out! Literally loads of £50 notes. I can't remember the exact amount, but it was a lot of money. Wrapped round the notes was a message simply saying: "If you ever get fed up of retirement, give me a ring."

Was the man a prankster? None of this added up. Perhaps the money was counterfeit? I stopped at the services on the way home to examine it, to see if it was real. Holding them to the light, the notes looked fine to me. Naturally, the money was on my mind. I had never seen so many £50 notes, but still needed more convincing. I took the cash to the NatWest Bank in Alfreton, near where I was working, and asked them to check. A female cashier I knew told me every one of them was legitimate.

Happy days! But, of course, I wanted to know why the man had done that. I fought against myself for the next few days. Half of me was desperate to know what this was all about, the other half told me to leave well alone. There was room in my life for another challenge, if he was proposing something positive. I had no intention of stopping training but now I lacked an end goal. Without a fight to prepare for, it would be difficult to stay motivated.

I was also at a crossroads in my personal life. I've not gone into details about my first marriage, because that's not fair on others, but I knew by now it was falling apart. I was in in limbo land, not knowing where the future was taking me. So, a few days later I dialled the number on the note. "Mr. Sepede's residence," was the reply. That sounded posh. I have changed the names involved for obvious reasons.

I couldn't say who I wanted to talk to because there was no name on the note, but when I mentioned boxing he knew straightaway. Another man – I'm going to call him Carlos – came onto the line. "I didn't expect you to ring so quickly," he said, in a foreign accent I couldn't quite place. "Are you bored already or just curious?"

We chatted for a short while and he dangled a carrot. If I visited him, it could be beneficial for me – and wouldn't cost me anything. What was this all about? He told me he lived in Buckinghamshire and I could stay at his place for a few days, all at his expense. I said my car wasn't reliable enough for such a long journey and would travel by train. But no, he would send a car for me. How could I refuse? I told Val, but wasn't very specific. I didn't know what to expect myself! I said I had to be away from home for a few days – no more detail. We were used to spending time apart, so it was no big issue.

A Rolls-Royce pulled up at my door. It looked like a wedding car with a chauffeur also looking the part, and a long, strange journey followed. The driver was a very schooled, educated person. I tried several times to find out what was waiting for me. Each time I started talking, he skilfully shut me down and avoided the issue. He answered questions with questions and obviously knew his job well. Try as I might, I wasn't going to get any information or names out of this guy. I shut my eyes and got some sleep for an hour or so.

Eventually we went down a very long driveway and pulled up outside a mansion in the middle of nowhere. There were no neighbours in sight, that's for sure. A member of staff approached. He was in his mid-twenties, well dressed in a black suit and politely asked to take my luggage. He even addressed me as "sir".

The place was as special as I imagined from the outside. It had four floors, plus its own swimming pool and library. I'd never seen anything like it. I waited in the drawing room until Carlos entered and shook my hand. I recognised him. It was a bit of a shocker. I had seen him at boxing shows and knew who he was, but we had never talked properly.

He didn't say why I was there. We went horse riding, which I'd never done before, and we talked about this and that. I knew the score. He would come to the point when good and ready. In the meantime, he was teasing me by not being specific. No point asking him questions.

Next day Carlos and another man, who looked like his bodyguard, took me on a tour of the city of London. More new ground for me. I had boxed at the Albert Hall but hadn't the time nor inclination to take in the sights of the city. We walked down Carnaby Street and into Savile Row. I was fascinated by the artists and the buildings and noticed how many people Carlos knew. Many foreign people, in particular, said hello to him.

Carlos said he might be going to an event during my stay and asked if I would like to come with him. I asked what type of event it was and he told me it would be one I would be interested in. I had a shirt and tie with me, but he insisted on fitting me up for the occasion at a very posh male tailor. On display were top hats fit for Royal Ascot as we entered through flights of steps. I was measured up very, very precisely and efficiently – inside leg, outside leg, thigh, calf, the lot. I was asked to pick the fabric, but preferred to leave it in their more than capable hands. I was also bought some brogues.

We went back to London next day to pick up the suit, and there was no need to try it on in the shop. We knew everything would be spot on and back at Carlos's mansion, I found out that was so. It looked unreal. So perfect. Carlos talked more about "the event", saying it would be an interesting night for me. I said he hadn't told me what it was all about and he explained it was a "fisticuffs show, a boxing show with a difference." Now I was getting the idea.

He also said a few words about the £50 notes. He had followed the ups and downs of my professional career with interest and made some money out of me along the way. This was a token of his appreciation! He didn't press the subject and took me into the snooker room, where he gave me a good beating, before asking if I'd seen bare-knuckle fighting. When I said no, he revealed this was what we were going to see. It sounded interesting.

The venue was like a welfare club, a biggish place with a bar. The men on the doors were enormous, much bigger than me. Carlos introduced me to a couple of people, but didn't give their names, nor did they introduce themselves. I was too busy taking in my surroundings to take much notice.

The fights took place in an elevated circle rather than a boxing ring and the fighters didn't acknowledge their names when announced. This was strange. The fights were short – some less than a minute. There must have been 10 to 12 during the evening and between 150 and 200 people watching. They appeared well heeled; the hierarchy, if you like. I gather they included judges, police officers and people from the world of entertainment. I only instantly recognised one, but will keep his name to myself.

The fighters weren't well matched, size-wise, with very large men fighting smaller ones. There were no rounds as in boxing, but it was a fight to the finish with no draws. Either one man gave up or was knocked out. The rules were far different from boxing. Some fights were just bare- knuckle and in others you were allowed to kick, but they all had the same endings. The man signalled that he had had enough, or he was knocked out; in the circle, there was no referee.

It all seemed very cliquey. There weren't many ladies there, as you would expect at a boxing show, and cigar smoke wafted around. I got the impression some fighters weren't that bothered – they seemed to be there to make up the numbers. The next morning, at breakfast, Carlos asked me what I thought. "It was different," I replied. I was keen to know whether these fighters trained, as I wasn't very impressed with their fitness levels. I also asked whether it was illegal – that depended whether anyone was going to stop it, he said. I gathered that, considering the level of people in the audience, all bases were covered.

"Do you fancy having a go?" he said. That was the six-million-dollar question. He told me the money was good and, when he started talking figures, I agreed. I knew the score. I knew it from the start, really. He had brought me here to try to hire me as a bareknuckle fighter. That was fair enough and I felt free to say no. I said I needed time to think. I went back home the next day with thoughts racing through my head. I didn't know what to do until I thought about Dad. What would he do? He was very handy with his bare fists, an expert you might say. After a few days of hard thinking, I phoned Carlos with my answer. I was in!

I would have one fight and see how it went. Carlos agreed, reassuring me there would always be security to ensure we didn't get into trouble. I would be there to do a job. Although I'd been involved in a lot of things in my life, my slate was clear. Not many people on Hyson Green had a clean police record and that meant a lot to me. Dad warned that, if I ever brought trouble to his door, he would beat the hell out of me – and he would! I did things against the law but was clever enough not to get caught.

I asked him again if it was safe health-wise. He said there were plenty of medical people at the shows and, when extra help was needed, I would be taken straight to hospital, providing I didn't let them know how I had been injured. That didn't sound great.

Carlos was my point of contact, my manager if you like. He told me about fights and suggested opponents. We had an agreement and largely stuck to it. Our relationship was very professional. We didn't socialise together, apart from perhaps a meal after the fighting was over. For obvious reasons, that was always a fair way from the venue. I spent more time with him when fighting abroad, but he was usually surrounded by quite a few others.

Carlos gave me an insight into other fighters, although I picked up much of it myself. They ranged from teenagers to men in their seventies. Many trained for strength rather than speed and that's where I had an edge on them. My speed from the boxing ring never left me. Sometimes Carlos pointed out a fighter and suggested him as a future opponent. He had quite a few fighters under his wing and looked after me extremely well.

Carlos usually didn't reveal too much about his personal life. At one show abroad, a very finely dressed, attractive woman was flirting with him. He could also see me looking at her and asked if I liked her, before confiding: "I have a lot of loves in my life!" It came up in conversation that he was married. I think his wife was the woman I saw him with at the mansion – but I can't be sure. He wasn't a man to be trifled with.

I found out there were people higher than Carlos in the organisation. When we were abroad, he told me I needed to put on a particularly good show because someone special was coming to watch that night. When I asked who, he answered: "The man above me," and left it at that. It took this man all his time to say hello to me. I soon got the idea. Fighters were tools. We were never told much about the business as a whole.

As a doorman and security man myself, I spotted Carlos had protection around him most of the time – someone standing a few feet away or blending into the background. I knew what to look for from my own experience. My deal with Carlos was like this: if my purse was £2,000 from a fight, I'd take a couple of hundred and trust him to put the rest into the pot. Carlos said he could "grow the money". I never asked how, but I expected to walk away with a nice amount of money when I quit.

There were familiar faces and some new ones wherever we went. Women were still rare. It's one thing for a woman to watch a boxing show, but bare-knuckle is another matter. I wouldn't want a lady of mine seeing that kind of thing. There was plenty of money changing hands, but never cash. Business was done on the nod with hand signals and signs. Carlos was clever. He put a lot of money on my fights but always checked how I was. If I wasn't feeling so good, he was more conservative. I could respect the people involved in the business for getting themselves into that high circle; as for the fighters, I can't have respect for people I don't know and intend on doing me as much harm as possible.

I wasn't paid a retainer, but sometimes Carlos gave me expenses. For example, if my next fight was abroad, he provided money to cover my travel and other needs. I had a full-time job back home whilst I was bare-knuckle fighting and it was sometimes awkward getting time off. I was lucky to have exceptionally good gaffers. I let them know a little of my business, not enough to get me into trouble. I was forced to make up a fair few stories after I returned battered and bruised. I usually said something like I'd been involved in a big brawl and had come out second best.

In return, I made time up when I came back and was happy to work seven days a week. I kept as many of my holidays free as possible. I did everything I could to keep on the right side of my gaffers by doing them favours, so they were good to me. I threw sickies at times, which I hated doing. Sometimes Carlos and his friends asked if I needed any additional work. I said no because I already had the doors and close protection stuff.

My first fight was in England down south – I can't be more specific. I treated it very seriously. I was still very fit after finishing my professional boxing career, and trained very hard. News of the fights came directly from Carlos. He typically phoned up with the barest details. He had got a fight for me, maybe in two weeks or a month. The shortest notice was six days. Usually, I didn't have much idea about my opponent and was given only a rough guide of where it was taking place.

Carlos took care of all the arrangements and gave me more information nearer the time. My travel and accommodation, if needed, would all be sorted. If the fight was in Britain, I usually travelled by train and he took me to the venue from the station; if abroad, I saw him at the airport. That might be on the day of the fight or the day before.

The venues were widespread. I fought in Buckinghamshire, Southend, Newcastle, Yorkshire, Nantwich and Scotland and, further afield, in Kenya, Italy, Germany, France, Belgium, Turkey and Austria. That's not a full list as my memory is a bit hazy. My experience in Kenya was one I won't forget. All I could see in the audience were teeth and eyes; it was a dark, dark place. I had a real handful in the ring, coming up against someone much smaller. He was a Thai kickboxer with feet like lightning.

He knocked me from pillar to post, kicking me on the side of the head. I had real problems with him until he made his one big mistake. He bent his foot down to give himself extra leverage to kick, giving me a split second to pull his leg up and whack him on the chin with a left hook. As he collapsed in the sand, I snapped his leg for good measure.

I had a hell of a lot of bruises to show after that. Most of the short time I was fighting him, I tried to keep my distance to soften the impact of his kicks. But I've never come across anyone as quick as him. I was black and blue with injuries to my face, shoulder, knees and thighs and was limping for weeks afterwards.

During my 13 years of bare-knuckle fighting, I never knew what was coming next. I might go six months without a contest, then get two or three in quick succession. My trick was always training properly, then step it up a notch when I had a fight. I got the impression some of my opponents were mainly in it for the pay day and didn't put the work in.

I had broken fingers, dislocated elbows, cracked ribs, teeth missing, broken toes and shut eyes – and I got off lightly. As for the hospitals, I lost count of the number of times I said I'd fallen off garage roofs. I also varied the hospitals I went to and memorised a few different names and national insurance numbers, so I didn't give too much away about what was really happening to me.

I didn't have much choice if Carlos offered me a fight, although he asked rather than told me. He checked if I was in good condition and up for a fight and I never let him down. My martial arts background helped, as I used a mixture of martial arts and boxing skills to sort out my opponents. The fights were always short compared with a boxing match. I'd say my longest was about six to seven minutes, and the shortest lasted 15 seconds. I pushed this guy backwards, then landed a bullseye on his chin and he was down and out in less time than it took him to get into the ring.

I wasn't too keen at first but started to really enjoy it. Once one opponent was dispatched, I was looking forward to felling the next. I was in a dangerous place, both mentally and physically, becoming very driven by winning. I was getting worried about myself, because this was nothing like the sport I had been brought up with. There was nothing sporting about it all. I'm toning it down here because I don't want to go into the full details, but this was do or die. Either me or my opponent was going to take a battering.

It wasn't like boxing in the sense of knowing about my next opponent or viewing footage, so I could work out my tactics. All I had to go on was the occasional time Carlos mentioned a name and I remembered him from one of the previous venues. Mostly I hadn't a clue who I was fighting. I thought bare-knuckle fighting was ensuring my financial future, whilst becoming increasingly aware of the risks involved to my health. As I was still trusting Carlos with the lion's share of the money, I knew I was stacking up a large pot. But how long could I keep it going for?

As with the Thai boxer, I had some contests which genuinely scared me and brought home how dangerous this was. Whilst I was winning, things were good. But the longer I continued fighting, the more I thought about the possibility – or probability – that one day I would be on the wrong end of a serious beating. There was another red flag in one fight when I got hit flush in the chest and felt my body almost explode, with pain spreading throughout the top half. It felt like a heart attack.

Somehow, I kept my opponent at a distance before grabbing him round the throat and hanging on for grim death as I almost put him to sleep. Never have I felt so pleased in my life to finish a fight. I was on the verge of passing out as I made my way back to the dressing room. That kind of incident stays in your mind and leaves scars. It increased my fears that next time I wouldn't be able to get out of such an awful situation. I wasn't just battered and bruised; I was hurting badly on the inside.

That was one time I told Carlos I was genuinely hurt. It didn't feel any better two weeks later and I went to hospital reporting I'd had an accident at home. I was told I had jarred myself and was suffering from internal bruising. I began to think then my body was telling me it was time to walk away, but vowing "never again" wasn't enough. I was soon wanted for another fight, and so it went on.

A couple of fights later, I realised I had gone through about 35 brutal contests – some against people who should never have been matched with me, others who seriously worried me –over a number of years. I told Carlos it was time for me to quit. I was fighting young blokes many years my junior and it was taking more and more out of me.

I was now going out with Lucy and that also played a part in my thinking. I probably had three or four more fights whilst I was with her and the reason I didn't tell her about bare-knuckle fighting back then was to protect her. I didn't want her to become known to the people running those events. These guys know everything about you – and they use it. I wanted to keep Lucy to myself.

I'd kept my nose clean with Carlos and done everything to be on good terms with him. I never turned down a contest, however difficult or inconvenient it was; I hadn't complained and had largely kept my problems to myself. I told him I had accumulated a lot of money and he agreed. But he explained how awkward it would be for me to get out, because of the people above him in the organisation. I found out some fighters were blackmailed into staying. It was made clear that, if they quit, videos would be released of their illegal fights and they would be in trouble with the law.

Carlos promised: "I have magic in me that I can work."

But first he needed a favour – a couple more fights before I quit. He showed me a photograph of my first opponent. I looked at what Carlos described as an "awesome beast, who is empty inside." The last thing I wanted was to fight this man, but Carlos said he had a lot of money riding on it. I still didn't want to go through with it until Carlos added: "Unfortunately, Steve, this is going to happen. I have done things for you. This one, and one more and it will end." I asked if that was definite and he said: "Yes, I can assure you, you can go with no repercussions."

The fight took place in Scotland. He was a British bloke in his late twenties, a lot taller than me and with a chin like granite. I hit him on it many times and he smirked. When he hit me a couple of times, it felt like a rock. I realised I couldn't afford to hang around – I needed to get this won or I could end up in big trouble. I won that fight in a naughty way. I hit him on the chin and put my arm up in the air as a distraction, before punching and kicking him in the balls. He squealed with pain. I could easily have finished him there and then as he was in no position to defend himself. I felt bone on bone in that contest. It was frightening.

Now I had one more fight. I trusted Carlos on this – I had no reason not to. I told him I had been hurt and was glad this was going to be the very last time. My last fight was back in England. I went for a walk during the afternoon because I wanted to relax and take in what was about to happen. When I first started bare-knuckle fighting, I didn't like it. Then I liked it too much. Now I couldn't wait to get out.

I got that last fight done and dusted and in total, I fought 41 times. I won 40, and the other was abandoned. I was on top in the fight, knocking my opponent all over the place, when the doors flew open as the venue was being raided. I looked at Carlos and followed him and his minders out as quickly as possible. Everyone ran like headless chickens. I saw police officers in uniform and what I presumed were officers in civvies. Luckily, they made one mistake.

They all entered the building but left nobody outside to cut off our escape. We ran to Carlos' car and disappeared into the night. It was a particularly hairy moment when I was on the verge of getting out of bare-knuckle fighting. We had been very close to falling foul of the law right at the last. Luckily, we heard no more about it.

All I needed to do was settle up with Carlos. He told me he needed to be away for a while but would sort out my money on his return. I tried to contact him six weeks later, with no success. Then I tried him at home on his private number. When his chauffeur Max answered, I explained who I was and said I wanted to speak with Carlos. "No, cannot speak," he answered in broken English. I told him it was very urgent, but he said the same thing again. I asked why and he said: "He is dead!"

I thought he meant the phone line was dead, but he added: "He is dead. Mr. Carlos is dead." This wasn't making any sense. I asked how he had died, or had he been killed? But I didn't get a proper answer. I phoned a few more times over the next week, but always got the same response.

Soon afterwards I pieced together the small bits of information I had about the people above Carlos over the years and flew over to Sicily, hoping to find someone who could get me my money. I'd been there a couple of weeks and was still asking around without getting anywhere when I was given a very direct message. I was in a public toilet when a huge guy stood alongside me and asked if I was Steve. I said I was. "Time for you to go home," the guy said.

I looked outside where another very large, threatening man was staring at me. "You go home, you live!" the first man added. I'm not easily scared, but this was no time to argue. The graveyard is full of have-a-go heroes and I didn't want to join them. I got out of that godforsaken hole as quickly as I could.

I knew then I had lost a lot of money – I estimate my losses at £180,000 – and there was never any prospect of me being paid what I was owed. Of course, I was angry, very angry. I put my body on the line 41 times and only got a fraction of the money agreed. I don't think I will ever find out what really happened to Carlos. But I have a fair idea. Unlike him, I got out of bare-knuckle boxing alive.

It took me a while to come to terms with what happened. It was an experience – a very expensive one. But there was nothing I could do about it because I was out of my league with these guys. For the sake of my health, I had to let it be. I know what would have happened had I pursued the matter any further. I had gone to Sicily out of hope, but inside I knew it was going to be an uphill struggle. After a few days, I realised nothing good was going to come of it. I was only going to get more and more grief.

It was a case of here today, gone tomorrow. There was no one I could turn to. All communications were cut. I spent many nights tossing and turning in bed, thinking everything over in my mind, until I came to the point where I more or less put it out of my head. Did Carlos mislead me? I don't think so. He was the one person I could trust in the world of bare-knuckle boxing. My feeling is that when he died, the money died with him.

He got the money safe, so nobody else knew about it – good whilst he was alive, but a bad thing now he was dead. I try not to think about him now because it reminds me about the money. I'm never going to get an answer, so what's the point? The money would have made a big difference to me. I was building a nest egg for the rest of my life. But what I never had, I don't miss.

Up to that point, from my early reluctant days at the Nottingham School of Boxing to my last bare-knuckle brawl, fighting had always been a big part of my life. But after finishing bare-knuckle fighting, I piled weight on and stopped training for a while. I wasn't bothered. I had a job, was going out with Lucy and working on the doors. I was going back to a 'normal' life. Or perhaps having a normal life for the first time?

6

THE TRAMP AND THE SURGEON

We can't always choose what happens to us or how one incident changes our life for ever. I suffered an horrendous accident at work when I was 50 years old. I've been through a lot in my 65 years and this was one of the most devastating, physically and emotionally. It took me to the brink of death itself, so now I know how precious health and fitness really is.

I'm sure I wouldn't be standing here now as a world-record-breaking boxer if I hadn't gone through that horrible agony. I was in a limbo period in my life after finishing bare-knuckle fighting, and working for Tarmac-owned Charcon Tunnels when my new world collapsed.

Working there as a concrete manufacturer suited me fine. I enjoyed being with down-to-earth people who worked with a smile on their faces. I have always thrived on physical work and I was left alone to get on with the job. The job was well paid and on my doorstep in Kirkby-in-Ashfield. Part of my role was to fill in the blow holes on the concrete segments and help with the manufacturing side.

I'd been there for about a year when disaster struck in August 2006. Everything happened so quickly and was totally out of my control. I turned round to pick up the bucket to get out the soft concrete when the segment fell towards me.

I was trapped. There were moulds directly in front and behind me, so I had nowhere to go. The concrete segment, which weighed about a tonne and a quarter, fell with a dead thud onto my right foot. It instantly flattened my steel toe cap boots and caused the worst pain I have felt in my life. I know how to deal with physical pain, and didn't yelp or scream. But this was serious.

I was thinking: "Oh God, the pain," and needed help quickly. All the workers were well spread out in a factory the size of an airplane hangar. "Can someone help me?" I shouted. No response. "Someone help me... I'm trapped!"

I couldn't even look around as I was rooted to the spot. I tried to get my left hand far enough down under the arch to lift the segment off my foot. No chance. The terrible pain in my foot limited my movement. I shouted louder and louder; I was trembling, fighting to stay conscious.

It was a full 10 minutes before my workmate Jason walked towards me. "What's the matter, Steve?" he shouted. "I'm trapped!" I replied. He had no idea what a mess I was in until he got much closer. "Oh my God," he said, going into shock. Now I had to deal with his trauma.

"Sit down on that bucket, take a deep breath and get yourself together," I said. "Now, get up, f*** off and bring that overhead crane over here." Jason ran for help and half-a-dozen others heard his cry. They carried iron bars to lift the segment. Moving my foot was torture. Even the slightest movement added to the pain.

Dave Bell, one of my closest colleagues, and Gary, a former boxer, were among those who helped me move my leg over and away from the segment as excruciating pain shot up my leg and into my groin. Dave put his arm around me, asking: "Is there anything I can get you, buddy?"

I asked for a seven-pound lump hammer with a long handle. "What do you want that for?" he asked, looking puzzled.

"To knock the f*** out of that segment!" I replied. He couldn't believe I was joking. I had to, because I was feeling less than good. I was helped towards the hanger door where almost the whole workforce had gathered. They sat me down, saying they needed to get me straight to hospital. There was talk of calling an ambulance before it was decided to take me to nearby King's Mill Hospital in an open-back Transit van.

I arrived at hospital about half an hour to 40 minutes after the accident and I was so relieved to be there. One of the lads got me a wheelchair to put me in the queue for accident and emergency, where a triage nurse said I needed to be seen straightaway and I was wheeled past other patients into X-ray. That was about all I remember. Next thing I knew I was waking up on a ward high on morphine several hours later. The medication must have knocked me out.

Looking down at my foot, I saw something big and white. It must have been a cast. Although still heavily medicated, I knew what had happened to me. Mr. Moore, one of the head managers at Charcon Tunnels, was at my bedside. "I can't believe what has happened – I'm so sorry," he said. He was genuine, saying the accident wasn't my fault. I eventually found out why it happened. There should have been four pieces of wood for the concrete to sit upright on safely – there were only two or three. I know who was responsible, but that's now all water under the bridge.

Lucy was working at the hospital when the accident happened. I needed to be extra strong. She looked devastated, bless her. "I'm alright, there's nowt wrong," I said. Nothing could have been further from the truth, but I was doing my best to calm her down whilst shaking inside.

There were strange events to contend with as I tried to come to terms with the accident during three or four days in hospital. There were no beds available on any other ward, so I was put with patients I can only describe as being 'not quite there'. One night, a Lurch-like figure hovered over my bed saying "Hello." Nothing I said made any difference, as he kept on saying it. "Bugger off!" I told him. Another time I might have thought this was funny; this wasn't one of them. I wasn't in the best of moods with the staff either. "I'm trying to rest and I've got Lurch saying: 'Hello' and a guy in an epilepsy hat threatening to headbutt me."

Lucy asked if I was settling in. "No, I'm surrounded with nutters," I said. "Ah well, you should fit in okay then," she joked.

Feeling down and in a lot of pain, I wanted to know what the medics could do. During a follow-up visit, a specialist said I was suffering from 'complex regional pain syndrome'. That's code for hurts like f***.

The cast was soon replaced with a grey air boot. That was less claustrophobic. I had never been afraid of anyone in my life but have been plagued ever since by a fear of being closed in. From frequent nightmares to pushing the panic button during MRI scans, I've lived with the mental health issues as well as the physical effects.

Even in my state, I wasn't going to sit in the house all day. After a week, I wanted to go to work and Mr. Moore arranged a lift. He understood why I preferred to come back but would have to put me in the office. He said he didn't mind if I sat there all day talking. I told him there was no way I'd do that.

My day started hours before work. I got up at five in the morning to take my medication. I was on three lots – gabapentin, morphine and ketamine, a horse tranquilliser that is even stronger. Within minutes, I was out on my feet, my head spinning. It was all I could do to grab the collar of Yoyo, my 13-stone French mastiff, to scramble onto the settee. Sometimes I made it, others I didn't, but that dog was my helper. I was in no condition to face the world for another three hours.

The medication never touched the pain but took my mind off it in a way. I was no longer myself. I was all over the place, forgetting even important things and not eating properly. Any sleep I could get then was a help as bedtime was so difficult. Getting my leg in the right position was impossible. We tried putting it in a cage and sleeping with my leg outside the bed, but nothing eased the pain.

Then there was the problem of going to the loo. I did everything I could to avoid the need but when nature called, I had the complications of removing the boot and somehow hobbling to the toilet. Lucy offered to help, but this was something I needed to do by myself. Then I had to put the boot back on and pump it up. This was awkward, painful and took a long time. It was better than using a commode, though – that was for older people.

I told Lucy a few more white lies. I assured her I was beginning to feel a bit better when, if anything, I was worse. Mr. Moore knew I wasn't really fit enough to work but did everything he could. I even had a lady to make me coffee – Michelle was lovely. I called her "Yum Yum." She looked after me like a sister, helping me settle into a new way of working, and I soon became good at it. I did technical drawings of the segments and was given a health and safety task going to all the offices. They soon regretted it though as I was very thorough and wouldn't give green labels to many items that weren't PAT tested. After being taken to another area, a woman called Jackie said she couldn't give me anything too demanding.

The company had to be careful nothing else happened to me. Putting nuts on bolts all day, the dark thoughts started. I couldn't believe life had come to this. The thought of doing this for the rest of my life didn't appeal. Even stuffing turkeys into separate bags for the 200 workers failed to get me into the Christmas spirit.

I worked there for another year before there was a round of redundancies. I was given the nod that the local factory was going to close and moved to another concrete company. I thought I was losing my life. Work aside, I didn't want to go anywhere. Our social life was crumbling because it was too tiring and I couldn't take risks with my foot. Lucy put up with a lot, and I mean a lot. At least I found out who my real friends were. Those who were only interested when we could go out soon dropped off the radar.

I saw specialists everywhere – in Mansfield, Nottingham, Derby, even Harley Street in London. I knew the latter were the top dogs and hoped they could give me some hope. But the message was always the same: it was unlikely I would walk again unaided. The best I could hope for was to hobble around with a stick. I respected the medics and believed what they told me. I think they did what they could for me.

But it was very hard for me after living a very active, physical life. I wasn't used to it and it had a big impact on my mental health. I kept things to myself as much as possible but was beginning to have stupid thoughts. I went through a time when I thought I would be better off without my foot.

After all, it was dead and racked with pain. Perhaps having it amputated would help? I was deadly serious. Lucy said the decision would probably not be mine and I should talk about it with the medics. They made it clear that, in my case, it wouldn't. That was another possible door closed.

Finally, I made a decision. I couldn't cope with the medication any longer. I'd been on it for four months and was constantly in pain. I needed that crap out of my life. It was still making me nauseous and sick for no reason. I discussed it with Lucy and she said I should talk it over with my GP. My appointment was a few weeks later. The doctor, who knew me well, said: "Be very, very careful how you do it. You need to be weaned off bit by bit. Have you thought about when you want to start?"

"Three weeks ago!" I answered. He asked the question again, thinking I'd misunderstood. I told him that I had come off all the medication cold turkey three weeks earlier. He was shocked, but I was already feeling better in myself. It certainly hadn't been easy but what kept me going was knowing I could live with the pain if I could feel myself again. I went for a couple of check-ups to ensure I was alright and the GP said: "You are an amazing man. I don't know anyone else who could have done that."

I did much the same thing over the boot. The only way to find out how my foot would be without it was to take it off. And that's what I did. It was a struggle and I fell down many times but, with the help of my sticks, I kept going. But dark thoughts again crowded in on me. Was this all

I had to look forward to? Hobbling around in pain, doing menial jobs, feeling like my life was over?

I had another idea. I wanted a car again. Driving had been out of the question after the accident but perhaps I could get round this. I knew the car I wanted and I got it – a Mitsubishi Pajero 4x4 automatic. Now I was mobile again.

I'd forgotten one important thing. To drive an automatic, you use your right leg and rest your left. It was my right foot that was the problem. I wasn't going to be beaten. It was very awkward and probably illegal, but I managed to manoeuvre my left leg onto the pedal instead. I wasn't intending to drive stupid distances. I just wanted to get out and about, including to my mate's house at Hucknall.

I was coming back from seeing him along Annesley Road when I saw police ahead stopping cars. "Oh shit, I'm in trouble," I thought and indicated right down a side road. My luck wasn't in, however, as the road led to a field and I was stuck. I stayed there for three hours, hoping the police would be gone when I went back onto the main road. Eventually I hobbled out of the car to look. A woman spotted me looking in distress and asked what I was doing. She told me the police had gone two and a half hours ago!

Nothing was lifting my mood, though, and I now realise mental health problems can happen to the strongest guys in the world. Nobody is immune. I still felt useless and didn't want to be a bugbear. I wouldn't have wished the physical and emotional pain I was going through on anyone. Nobody deserved this. When I say I had suicidal thoughts, I'm not being over dramatic. Life and death for me had become borderline. And one day it came to the crunch.

I had planned how I was going to end it. I had access to guns if I wished and got one off a friend of a friend. I drove to a spot near the Goose Fair site in Nottingham and sat there early in the morning with crazy, jumbled up thoughts racing through my head. Sobbing and sweating, I pulled the window down to get some air. I was facing the ultimate. The gun was in my hand and I put it in position at the side of my head.

This was it.

Suddenly, the gun was snatched out of my hand. Trapped with my own thoughts, I hadn't seen anyone or anything. I got out of the car. It was a tramp! My first thought was to chase after him – as best I could – and slam him down. I was going to kill him. Then came the realisation: "This guy has saved your life." Instead of attacking him, I took him to Trowell services on the M1 and bought him a meal.

He was intelligent and well-spoken, yet unshaven and filthy. He talked with me for some time and got me to promise I wouldn't kill myself. I was beginning to take in what had happened. This guy could have been killed doing what he did. I asked if he wanted taking anywhere, but he preferred to be left at the services. I don't think I ever knew the name of that man who did me the ultimate favour.

That experience made me realise what I had left. I got rid of the gun and have never been back to that state in my head again. Now I'd say to anyone feeling like that – for God's sake, get help! Don't do what I did and try to keep everything to yourself. Sometimes we can't do it all by ourselves and need friends or specialist help. I'd kept all this from Lucy and had to tell her. But I still didn't do so straightaway.

Afterwards I went for counselling at Mansfield Hospital where they sent me to another place in the town. I won't say this would work for everyone; the key is you must want to

In the arms of my dad and inspiration, Bernard. Below: Dad in our version of Arkwright's shop

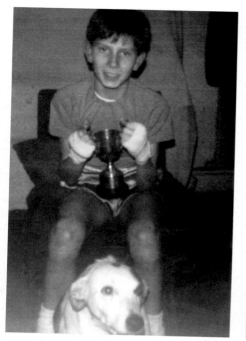
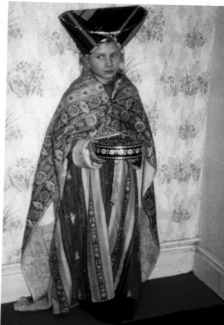

Me, aged 11, with an early trophy and our dog Hammer; and as one of the three wise men

Jackie Turpin was one of my victims as an amateur

Above: With my parents on my first wedding day. Below: At the wheel of the Mark 1 Batmobile

Above: Displaying my Guinness Book of World Records certificates and my championship belts.
Below: My wife Lucy and I pose for the camera with our French Bulldog, Bentley *(Mansfield Chad)*

Clockwise from top: With my team before the world title fight with German giant Andreas Sidon (*Mansfield Chad*); Lucy and I with my late friend and former snooker star Willie Thorne, RIP; The age gap caught up with me when I was beaten by Jody Meikle at Shirebrook Leisure Centre (*Nicola Parker Photography*); Being presented with an award for boxing by the mayor of Mansfield, Tony Egginton

I was well on top against Andreas
Sidon before injury disaster struck
(Nicola Parker Photography)

0096

SAOIRSE PROMOTIONS
PRESENTS

**STEVE WARD
(ENGLAND)
VS ANDREAS SIDON
(GERMANY)**

SATURDAY 15TH JULY
DOORS OPEN 7PM

£50.00

SAOIRSE PROMOTIONS PRESENTS

**STEVE WARD (ENGLAND)
VS ANDREAS SIDON (GERMANY)**

**WORLD BOXING CONFEDERATION VETERANS
CHAMPIONSHIP OF THE WORLD**

SATURDAY 15TH JULY 2017
DOORS OPEN 7PM, BOXING STARTS 8PM
MANSFIELD CIVIC QUARTER
CHESTERFIELD ROAD SOUTH, NG19 7BH
www.bethlehemboxing.com

9600

£50.00 VIP RINGSIDE TABLE

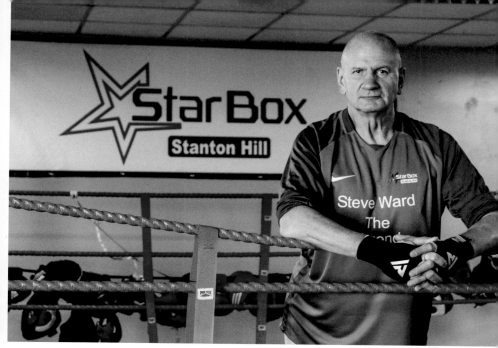

I am so fortunate to be able to train at Starbox very close to home *(Richard Markham Photography)*

For Queen and country: Action from my final fight against Adrian Parlogea, when I won the world title with a first-round knockout at Mansfield Rugby Club (*Nicola Parker Photography*)

get better. Whatever help is available, the decision is yours. You need to come to the point where you are ready for change. Following counselling, I started to feel more confident in myself and wanted to do things, so I began going down to the gym and talking to friends. I went to the washroom one day and was followed in by a Chinese guy I knew from martial arts. He said: "Steve, your foot is so, so, so bad. But you are so fast... my uncle says he can put it right."

"Put what right?" I asked.

"Your foot!" he said. "He is a surgeon and doctor and he can put it right. He wants to do it for you."

"Where is your uncle?" I asked, imagining yet another trip to Birmingham, London or Liverpool.

"He is in Hong Kong," he said. I thought he was kidding, but no. He was a clever guy and wouldn't let it go, asking me whether I wanted to do it.

"I'll chat with my wife," I answered. We arranged to meet the following week.

Lucy was great. She told me in no uncertain terms that it was my decision. Whatever I decided, she would back me 100 per cent. I couldn't have asked for better support. My decision to go to China was two per cent based on believing he could get me walking again and 98 per cent because he offered hope where there was none. My intuition told me I needed to take a chance.

I needed to fly to Kowloon and naturally this was going to be a paid job. The price I was quoted was a modest £5,000. I spoke to the surgeon on the phone a couple of weeks later. He didn't pressurise me. He said I should only do it if I was going into it wholeheartedly, otherwise it wasn't worth it. Yes, he was confident he could help me but there were endless ifs.

The surgeon said I was a very trusting man. "No, I'm a desperate man," I replied. I said I had tried every avenue; this wasn't my big hope, but my next hope. When I asked how we were going to play this, all he said was fly to Hong Kong and let him know where I was staying.

"You will be fine," he promised in broken English. "You pay the money and it is not a problem. Don't worry about it, we will come to you." There was nothing about what they intended to do, or how long it would take. Just a general promise he could help.

I knew the score. Whatever this guy was doing was unofficial. That only added to the risk of going to China, almost the last place I wanted to go anyway. There were endless dangers and uncertainties, but I would have done almost anything to be mobile and never to wear that boot again. My depression was already starting to lift. I felt better thinking something might be done.

I bought my ticket to fly to China and flew out on May 21, 2010, with no idea how long I would be there. It could be weeks, maybe months. I had asked Lucy to find me somewhere to stay whilst I spent the early days going to clinics. My priority was to keep it cheap.

I wasn't going to spend a lot of time there other than sleeping. She went online and found the King's Mansion Hotel. It was only £132 a week, and the photos looked good. The problem was that they weren't of that hotel!

After arriving at the airport, I got a cab to the hotel. Suddenly it stopped and the driver signalled to what looked like an arcade on the other side of the road. I was greeted by the worrying sight of a large group of pimps carrying guns, surrounded by 30 or 40 girls. Some weren't wearing anything on top; others weren't wearing very much at all.

Welcome to China, Steve! This wasn't looking good. The cab driver wasn't doing any more; it was left to me to get my luggage out of the car and run the gauntlet of this weird crowd of people. To make me feel even more vulnerable, I was wearing a money belt with my money for the operation and treatment and more for the trip. I was powerless if they turned on me.

As I walked towards them, it became obvious they weren't going to move. There was only one thing for it – push my way past them as discreetly as possible. That's what I did, and they didn't come after me. Phew, that was close! Now I needed to find the hotel. That wasn't easy. There were shops everywhere and no sign of the King's Mansion.

I tracked down a Chinese guy who spoke a bit of English. "Come, follow me," he said. We disappeared down an alleyway, coming to a sign that was in English as well as Chinese – the King's Mansion. "No, no, no!" he said. "I am going to a better place." No thanks, mate. I had no idea where he was taking me. But then again, perhaps I should have listened.

Walking into reception, there was an eight-foot cut out shutter down to the counter. "What you want?" was the greeting.

"I'm booked in," I tried to explain.

"You not booked in," he insisted. The last thing I needed, at three o'clock in the morning after a tiring flight, was an argument.

"Pay money!" he said. I told him I had already paid money. "No, you pay money!" he insisted. Two big tough men appeared at the side of me, opening their jackets slightly so I could see their guns. I then gave him a second payment for £132 and he led me to my room. I saw a half-finished building, steel reinforcements and pillars. None of this was on the photos!

"Your room," he said, getting out a big key. Oh my God, this didn't look good. Lucy had booked a double room with plenty of space to rest my foot. This was small and dingy, with an orangey-yellow light. The bed was tiny and, at first, I couldn't even see the toilet. When I found it, it was a toilet and shower combined. This was awful.

Worse was to come. My question about air conditioning – a necessity in temperatures of 40 degrees Celsius plus – was met by the man pointing towards a non-existent window. Sitting on a bed no more than 20 inches wide, I came across the last straw – a cockroach.

Yes, I was tired, but I needed to get out of there and find somewhere proper. "Lucy, what have you done?" I thought. It wasn't her fault. But this was no king's mansion, that's for sure. I hobbled out of the hotel with no idea where I was going. But I soon found the Kowloon Hotel, which was totally different. It was a lovely place, much more expensive but good value for money. They gave me the only remaining room – a suite with a fridge full of alcoholic drinks, a big oak writing desk and a king-size bed. Most importantly of all, it felt safe. I wouldn't need to sleep with one eye open here. I went to the King's Mansion to ask for my money back. Nothing doing. Fortunately, Lucy managed to withdraw the initial payment, so we only paid them once.

I sat in bed with all sorts of thoughts going through my head. What had I got myself into? I was thousands of miles from England and anyone I knew. Anything could happen to me here, but it was too late. I had come this far – no choice now but to go through with it.

I phoned the surgeon very early to tell him where I was

and sure enough, two people came to collect me. They also spoke in broken English I could barely understand. I asked if I needed to bring anything with me. They said no. They took me to a clinic of some sort for an X-ray, where I was asked if I was allergic to anything. I also remember going to a type of hospital and being injected. They kept taking me to different places during the day for tests then back to the hotel when I was finished.

In some ways, my stay in China was about my mind as much as my foot. We have an image of Chinese people being very robotic and state controlled, but I found them very warm as well as organised. Nursing staff and doctors seemed like hotel workers – anything I wanted, they got it for me. Each morning a group of 20 local pensioners walked into the grounds and the music started. I watched as they did an hour of Tai Chi-style martial arts. Then it was my turn to do the same with a nurse.

I got talking to an old man I knew as Lee Li, who referred to me as "Steve, the fighter." He was a great chap, 94 years old and still as fit as I was. He worked as a civil servant for the British before the revolution, then lost his family in the war with the Japanese, was thrown into a labour camp and half starved. Yet, despite suffering all these things, all he did was smile.

I really respected this man. I told him all about my life, boxing, bare-knuckles, money and why I was in China. We became good friends and spent hours together talking. When he asked why I had quit boxing and was no longer a fighter, I said I was "too old... past it as we say in the UK." He laughed and said I was only as old as my mind, which felt about 102! I had physical problems and my mind was ill too. He explained how he kept his mind young with exercise and reading. A good walk cleared his mind, helping him to see the bigger picture. I began to understand what he was saying and when we said goodbye, I thanked him for his help. "Giving help, means you have to use it," he replied. That I did after I returned to England.

I had been in China for about a week when the surgeon said: "Big day tomorrow." It must be operation day! I was collected from the hotel at four o'clock in the morning and taken here, there and everywhere. Finally, I was put into a gown and injected. I vaguely remember going through a door and that was it. Next thing I woke up and the first person I saw was a nurse or cleaner. The surgeon walked in wearing a suit and asked how I felt. I said I was tired and asked if he had done what he wanted. "Yes," he said. "Tricky, not big."

That sounded good. But what next? I needed to stay the night then go back to the hotel, where he suggested walking up and down Nathaniel Road to exercise my foot. Bloody hell, that road must have been a couple of miles long. It almost killed me walking up and down it. And that wasn't even half the story. Being streetwise from my years on the doors, I know when people are following me. Here I was easily identifiable as someone of a different colour, probably English or American, and therefore having some money.

I put my suspicions to the test by limping over a crossing and then going back again – and, yes, they were still on my tail. They weren't so keen to follow me when I walked into the front door of the police station and out the other side! China was a strange mixture of riches and poverty and some sights will live with me forever. Two people fighting over a little lizard, with the winner chomping it; sellers offering anything from watches to women dressed in coats, high heels and nothing else; ladyboys and other females suggesting I buy them a drink in return for "some fun." It was all going on.

About five days before my departure, the surgeon visited me at the hotel. He told me everything had gone well; the rest was up to me. He shook hands with me and left. The last I saw of a brilliant man. He told me never to give his name to anyone. I have kept my promise. Not even Lucy knows it. I know, though, that he was fantastic at what he did and was a people person. The best qualified people in Harley Street couldn't help me, but he did.

I was still in a lot of pain, but he said it would get easier. And he was right. It has got a lot, lot better although I still get pain in my foot from time to time. Five or six years ago I heard the sad news: "Your saviour is no longer with us." The surgeon, who gave me new hope and life, had passed away. I think about him often. Without his skill, much that has happened since would not have been possible.

They were hot, hot days and my foot was a pool of blood. Every day someone came to the hotel to change the dressing. All I needed now was to get home, and away from China – where my life had been changed for the better, but I always had to look over my shoulder. Steve Ward is an Englishman, get me out of here!

7

A TASTE OF GUINNESS

By Lucy Ward

Steve's foot injury was a terrible time in our lives. He always tries to play things down, but I knew how serious this was and it had a massive effect on his mental health afterwards. We were living in a one-bedroom flat opposite my parents and there were days when I took him there, so someone could keep an eye on him. He was deteriorating very badly on a cocktail of drugs. It wasn't nice to see and it put our relationship under a lot of strain. He was crying all the time, and just wasn't Steve.

Seven specialists, including some from Harley Street, couldn't do anything for him. We were told that, at best, he would always walk with a limp and need specialist shoes. This was awful for anyone, but particularly for someone who had been so physically active all his life. When he told me of the offer of hope elsewhere, I supported him 100 per cent. Either it was going to work, or it wasn't – but things couldn't get much worse. I think the idea of boxing again gave him something to aim for.

I get asked if I'm worried about Steve fighting at his age – and I'm not. I remember the first fight I watched when Steve made his comeback. I'd seen Barry McGuigan and Frank Bruno fight on TV but never been to a live boxing event before. I got there about half past five or six o'clock, and Steve told me his fight wasn't until 10pm. So, I had a few drinks and was on my feet for most of Steve's fight, becoming very loud. I found the atmosphere and buzz around the place very exciting.

Since then, I've calmed down because I know Steve can look after himself. He always gives at least as good as he gets and I know he'll be okay. I'm quite a statistical person and that's why I looked up the world record for the oldest boxer. I found out Dexter Dunworth, the record holder, was 53, and Steve was 54. So why not go for it? It proved to be a big job getting all the documents together to qualify for the Guinness Book of World Records, but it was well worth all the hard work.

I had already shocked some people by promising that, if I could walk again, I was going to fight again! At first, it was to give me a target – something to aim for. Approaching my mid-fifties, and having gone through the ultimate emotional and physical hell, I needed to look forward. But first, I needed to get out of China and be reunited with Lucy.

Step one was anything but simple. As I had noticed when I landed, Hong Kong airport is huge; two or three times the size of Heathrow. Hobbling along with my walking stick, with all directions written in Chinese, I got myself into quite a pickle. Finally, I came across someone who wasn't bad at English. "Other end!" he told me, softening the blow by saying he was walking in the same direction.

I did my best to look after my foot on the plane. It was still very sore and I probably overdid moving it. After a few hours in Dubai, finally we were on the last leg of the flight home and waiting to see the woman I love. Lucy was waiting for me at the airport, so I put on a good act.

Watching me limp with my walking stick, she said: "You're no better, you can't walk." I picked up the stick, snapped it in half and started walking towards the exit. Thrilled, Lucy asked if it was fully better. "No," I replied. "It hurts like hell, but I can walk on it. We're going to get through this."

I returned to Mansfield a different man. I had a calmness about me, a single-minded determination. I wanted to get married, finish at the concrete works, get back into the ring and box! Lucy looked at me as if I was a madman, then smiled. I kept telling her my plans and how I would bring them about. She kept nodding, smiling and laughing, so I asked her what she thought. "Well, you keep saying 'you this' and 'you that'," she said. "Remember it's 'us' now. You want to do it, then we will do it together and I mean together. First thing you need to do is pack up the job. Then you need to get fit and get the foot back on form."

She was right. This was about us, not me. My stay in China changed my life forever and, yes, it changed my relationship with Lucy. I came back to England strong enough and with the will to fight for my future. The nightmare after my accident was behind me at last.

I walked every day – still in a lot of pain – and a week later was back in the gym. It was my friend Gary Jackermelon's place in Blackwell, 15 to 20 minutes from home. He even gave me a key and said I could go there when I wanted. I was back where I belonged and felt great. But the best I could do was to stand beside the punchbag with my feet firmly anchored and throw a few shots.

It was one step at a time – but I was determined to push myself as hard as possible. I knew my foot was still bad but thought: "Okay, my foot is too sore for normal training, but perhaps I can walk?" It was five miles back home, so I gave it a try. Not a good idea. I was in agony and needed a couple of days of complete rest.

I knew I'd overdone it but wasn't giving up. Next, I tried the gym and walking half the distance. The foot throbbed a bit, but I could live with it. From there, I upped the number of walks before trying the five miles again. It was nothing like as sore as it had been the first time. After a couple of days, I had another go at the five-mile walk. Big mistake! Not enough recovery time. Undeterred, I kept trying. And once I did five miles, I did it twice, then three times, then four, then for a week.

One day I noticed Gary hadn't put all the stuff away, so picked up a rope and tried skipping. It was very, very painful. I went back on the bags, still pushing myself. Soon I was going to the gym, doing the bags, skipping for 20 minutes and walking five miles. At this stage, I was pushing to regain my physical fitness rather than thinking about boxing.

Soon I was able to do everything and noticed something very exciting – I wasn't even physically tired. Right, this was time to back up my brave words with actions and get back into the ring! I was still in quite a lot of pain with my foot but nothing like before. I was never going to be 100 per cent pain-free but could get physically fit enough to fight.

But, first, I needed every possible little advantage I could get. That's why I went to Geezers Palace in Norfolk and bought some calf-length boots to give my leg and foot extra support. Popular in the old days, they have since been replaced by Mike Tyson-style small shoes.

My mission was to prove to everyone who believed in me that I would do as I had said and box again. I was training on my own and, for the first time in my life, began to have niggly doubts in the back of my mind. I'd seen boxers be magnificent in training – hard punching, fast and accurate –

yet freeze and become slow and anxious when they got into the ring. Would that be the case with me?

I had doubts over what would happen to my foot when put under real pressure. Physically I felt better than ever. I was as fast as in my amateur days and had developed ways of increasing arm and shoulder strength. Rather than lifting the heaviest weights, I focused on repetition – lifting them again and again until I could feel my muscles burn. It would be the same on the other equipment; I worked until my body could literally take no more.

Life was getting better and better. Boosted by the operation and getting myself fit again, I was in a good position to move forward and Lucy and I decided to get married. Val and I had been divorced in early 2010 after living separate lives for years. She knew I had a new partner and my life had moved on. Unfortunately, my daughters refused to accept my new life but there was nothing I could do about that.

The big day came with one string attached. I told Lucy she'd have to arrange the wedding because I had a prior engagement I needed to prepare for – my comeback fight! We talked everything through. It all came out in one go – why I was going back into the ring and my feelings about Dad. I told Lucy how he showed people a photograph of me and predicted I'd be a world champion one day. I explained about Needham, the politics, the Smith fight and how I'd been denied my title.

At first, she looked at me as if I was mad, but eventually she smiled. She had grasped it. She knew my love for the sport; now she got why I needed to do it all over again. She said I would do it – I'd get my title. She had faith in me and would back me all the way. All I needed now was to get a fight, but nothing too heavy.

There was one more hurdle to overcome. Warm-up fights and sparring were useful, but didn't put real money in the bank. As Charcon Tunnels, the place where I had the accident, had closed, I moved to Evans Concrete at Pye Bridge. I also used my contacts from the doors and bare-knuckle days to get more close protection work.

I worked on film sets and with visiting rock groups. Sometimes it would be an airport run to collect a high-flying businessperson or hotel work guarding a celebrity or pop star. The money was good and you meet all kinds of people in that game. Just like the bare-knuckle world, you come across the rich and powerful, famous and arrogant as well as down-to-earth people who don't want any fuss. I enjoyed it and had some fantastic times.

I knew the Boxing Board of Control wouldn't allow me to box because of my age, so I approached my friend John Ashton, a promoter for the European Boxing Federation. John was a boxer I used to train with and had fought for British and European titles.

He was gobsmacked when I said I wanted to fight again and asked how old I was. When I said I was 54, he very politely suggested I should retire gracefully. I told him I was fit enough and invited him to watch me train and spar. He was so impressed he changed his mind, adding me to a show he was putting on at the Heritage Hotel in Derby.

Both Lucy and I have friends who go back many years. Their advice was nearly all the same. Most thought I was an old man with nothing left in the tank, who would be knocked out in the first round. I should hang up my gloves and put on my slippers before I looked a fool. I was hurt; Lucy was hurt and a little angry. But I kept it all in and channelled it. I would show them and then, if I failed, I could eat humble pie and retire for good. But no way did I want to go out an old loser. I was giving this everything.

John gave me the chance I needed and phoned with the details of my first fight in November 2010, barely six months after I had flown out to China. It wasn't what I had expected. Andy Myers was a 28-year-old from Leeds. He had a good record, was strong and had good ring craft. I did my research with Lucy and managed to view a couple of his fights. This boy was no pushover.

Lucy was concerned about his age and build. She asked if I honestly thought I could beat him; I said I would take him apart. I already had my tactics worked out in my head, so I stepped up the training and put together a good team in my corner. I was soon training seven nights a week.

But I have to admit that two or three weeks before my comeback fight, the doubts started to creep back in again. My mind was playing tricks on me. Was I fit enough? Fast enough? Could I get my timing right? Was I going to look a fool boxing in front of Lucy for the first time? After being away from the ring for so long, fighting was always going to be a mental as well as a physical exercise.

I needed to get that special feeling of a fight night fresh in my mind. I remembered what Lee Li said about using my mind. So, I went along when the workmen erected the boxing ring, and it helped me. I was now able to picture the fight, the ring, the crowd and my tactics.

I went for a long walk in the Derbyshire Peak District on fight day. I walked and walked; talking to no one. It cleared my mind. Lee Li had given me a nugget of wisdom; now I was using it for my benefit. Then I returned to the hotel for the weigh in. Myers didn't waste a second. He was shouting and mouthing like a kid. He said it was going to hurt him to put an old dog down and he was asking if I had a nurse to help me into the ring. What a clown.

The local Press tried to goad me to reply, but I waved them away. Trading insults wouldn't help. After the weigh in, Myers came right up to my face, calling me old this and old that. I could see it was getting to Lucy, who was watching, and enough was enough. I told him: "For every time you have used the word 'old', I will hit you with my right and every time you have insulted me, I will hit you with my left. See you tonight!"

We went back to our hotel room for light food and sleep, and the afternoon went slowly. I showered and felt fantastic; the best I had ever felt before a fight. Excitement ran through me like gold, setting me on fire. The corner team taped my hands and an EBF official looked me over in the changing room. Good to go! Shadow boxing in front of the mirror, I saw Dad standing behind me. Okay, I know you're thinking I'm mad; it was a trick of the light or my imagination. But I know what I saw and what I heard. He stood there in his suit and tie and said: "Go on son, this is your time." I knew there and then I had already won.

Officials tapped on the door – two minutes and I needed to be in the corridor. Myers insisted on going into the ring first and that suited me fine. Just the way I liked it. The noise of the crowd was growing as his music was played. That was it – Myers was out of my mind now. Not a name, nor a person, just a figure. I went through the tactics in my mind. Time to go.

Making my way through the crowd, music and lights, I blanked out shouts from friends and family. In the ring, I continued to warm up, avoiding contact with Myers. I ignored him as he mouthed off as the referee gave us his instructions, and I was straight at it. Going for the head with a good combination of right and left hooks.

Myers rocked and rolled on the ropes. Then I started on his ribs – hook, jab, hook, jab, uppercut. Myers seemed to have no response but had to find some way of saving himself. He threw a low punch that hit me hard in the testicles. The referee gave Myers a stern warning as I took a few deep breaths and was ready to continue. More punches to the head had Myers in trouble. Only the bell saved him from a first round stoppage.

Nobody in my corner said a word. They didn't have to. I had him and couldn't wait to finish him. Head shots, working to the ribs and then more uppercuts had the crowd on their feet. Myers' head rocked back before he delivered a second low blow.

The referee stopped the fight and threatened to disqualify him. Despite the pain, that was the last thing I wanted. But I was angry, very angry and forced Myers to take a standing count with a vicious right hook to the body. Unbelievably, the bell saved him again.

We touched gloves for the third and final round. I knew I had the fight won but there was no letting up. Then came the third low blow. Another break, another warning and I was well enough to continue. Hook after hook thudded into Myers' right-hand side. It was the 28-year-old who was spent. Not me.

When the final bell sounded, there was no doubt about the outcome. The crowd chanted "Wardy Legend, Wardy Legend" before the ref held my arm up. That was the first time I had been called a 'legend' and the title stuck – a boxer doesn't pick a name; he is given it. I fell to my knees, all the pain and frustration of the last few years flooding from me.

I was ecstatic. "Yes, yes, yes," I screamed. I had shown all the doubters who had told me to retire. Now I'd surely get a title shot.

Myers came into the dressing room to apologise for the low blows. I had closed his mouth and a few others. Myers had three cracked ribs and was hurting so much he could think of no other way to buy time than to cheat. He told me he had never been hit so hard or so fast and felt an idiot being beaten by a man more than 25 years older. Considering what he did, I didn't have much sympathy.

The pain from the low blows didn't go away. A couple of weeks after the Myers fight, I realised I had a seriously busted sausage. The leather protector cushioned some of the impact, but Myers had hit me hard and it wasn't nice. I was very, very sore and the pain when I went to the toilet made me wince. I went to the doctor several times and eventually to hospital. The only way they could ease my pain was to circumcise me. I was 55, for God's sake!

On the positive side, Dad was right. This was my time and I was going to make the most of it. In the days after the fight, all those who doubted me knocked at my door to congratulate me. I was polite, that's my way, but my mind was elsewhere – thinking of titles.

But first I had the perfect Christmas to plan. Lucy and I got married on December 18, 2010, on a cold, but beautiful, day at Mansfield Register Office. Lucy wore the wedding dress she had bought eight years previously but now the timing was right for us. There was a small gathering of family and friends at the ceremony, but the reception was another matter.

When we booked The Sherwood at Mansfield Woodhouse, we expected to cater for about 100. We sent out a lot of invitations, but most didn't reply. Then on the night they all came ... all 250 of them! Lucy and I managed to get something to eat about midnight. I never knew we had so many friends.

Meanwhile, news of my victory over Myers spread like wildfire. Nobody in the boxing business had wanted to know me, and now I was turning away offers. There were possible fights by the dozen, some carrying big purses which would have helped me and Lucy greatly. I didn't want to know. I only wanted a title fight and wasn't going to back down. In the past I had gone for money for the kids and made big mistakes. Now I was fighting for pride and, above all, a title for my father.

There was one name right at the top of my wish list; EBF Midlands cruiserweight champion Greg Scott Briggs. I con- tinually told John I wanted to fight Briggs, but he wasn't confident he could make it happen. To make sense of the obsession I had with Briggs, I need to go back to when we worked together at Pentos Office Furniture at Ripley. We talked a lot because we were both boxers, but I got the idea he patronised me because of my modest professional record. Every now and again, he had a dig. He was big headed, put- ting across that he was a boxing master everyone else should learn from

In 2008 I came across Briggs completely be accident when I took Lucy to a boxing show at The Royal Concert Hall in Nottingham. I was there to watch a friend Frankie Graham fighting, but noticed Briggs was on the bill and that was the night when he won his Midlands title. I was still hobbling with my foot injury and asked Lucy what she thought of him.

She said he had been too strong for his opponent and was

clearly impressed. I told her I wanted to fight him. I had a brief chat with Briggs afterwards and he was full of himself after winning the title. I congratulated him on his victory and made a mental note I was going to take his title off him.

When I got back into the gym, Briggs was never far away. When I hammered at the punchbag, I was fighting Greg Scott Briggs. Sometimes, if I didn't think I had done enough to beat him, I'd start the session all over again and be there for six hours. Again, the feeling was Briggs didn't rate me highly enough to want to fight me but I badgered and badgered John to keep asking. Eventually it happened in strange circumstances. We were both due to fight different opponents who then pulled out. John said he couldn't believe it and now we had a dilemma. I told him to ask Briggs to fight me and within an hour or so, everything was agreed.

Greg Scott Briggs had held the title for more than a year and defended it twice. This was going to be third time unlucky. I knew I could beat him. Briggs wanted to fight in his hometown of Chesterfield but there wasn't a big enough venue. His next choices were Leeds or Manchester. My camp wanted to keep it local, so all our fans could come. In the end, we agreed to return to the Heritage Hotel. I knew it well from the Myers fight; Briggs had defended his title there. Problem solved!

I was 54 years old and fighting a man who had been in the ring with former world heavyweight champion David Haye. Yet he used the same tactics as Myers, going all over Derbyshire telling everyone I was a pensioner. His words insulted me and the sport. No fighter should act that way, but I treated his nasty words similarly to Myers'.

I put them to one side, then used them as a focus when I needed to. Briggs made a big mistake as the local and national boxing world took my side. All kinds of people came to see me train, saying how disgusted they were with Briggs. I was going to teach him a lesson.

I had about four weeks to prepare and would have to work 12 hours a day to get my fitness to peak level. Then I hit on an idea. Tom was an old mate from my bare-knuckle days. A great lad, former military, who worked with me on close protection jobs, he had put all his money into a small farm in the north. I told him I was looking for a training camp, somewhere I could work hard and get ready. He was more than willing to help.

I needed to be away for three weeks and again Lucy supported me without question. "Off you go and do what you need to do'," she said to me. I know I couldn't have completed this journey without her love and backing. Tom greeted me with a sheet of paper – he had worked out a diet and training regime. He was planning to push me to the limits of my mental and physical endurance. Tom is a year younger than me, and I don't know what the hell he has inside him but it's not a human heart nor feelings. I thought I was fit until he started. After getting up at four o'clock in the morning to get the farm job done, he woke me an hour later for a six-mile run up and down hills. To add to the fun we had backpacks, one weighing 100lbs. He shouted at me all the way: "Run, you old bastard ... run, or I'll kick you all over the fucking hills." I was running on fumes.

Next, he opened the barn for an hour of circuit training including jump ups, sit ups, press ups, crunchies and squats and more. "Fifty pull-ups and we will eat," he promised as I begged for breakfast. For God's sake, I was on my knees. The hour's break with food from his special diet list was followed by bag work, speed ball, sparring and speed work with the odd break. More gym work followed, then it was time for the river!

It was a freezing cold river so strong the currents pulled my arse hair out. The task was to swim two miles from one side to the other and back. I shouldn't have complained that I was freezing. Tom's idea of how to warm up was to leave the car and have a three-mile run. When we got there, he said: "Shit, I've left the keys in the car. Can you run back and get them?" He told me not to be too long or I'd miss out on the evening meal. When I returned, Tom had found the car keys in his pocket. He was standing there with a plate of hot food, but first I had to do what he called "my little bit of paddling."

Those three weeks made me fitter than I have ever been in my life. I built up stamina and muscle like never before, as well as putting Lee Li's mental disciplines into practical effect. Tom made me sit down anywhere – field, river, bank or barn, it didn't matter – and not move. There was rain, hail, even snow at one point. At first, I couldn't understand why he was doing it, then it came to me. Sometimes in the boxing ring you must switch your mind off from the pain. Here, my legs cramped and went numb and my back ached, but my mind was elsewhere. It took great effort to sit there for hours; Tom had learnt it in his army training and could have sat for a full day with no problem.

Then he tapped me on the head and it was time for a run, or a swim, or the gym. I fell into bed thinking it was heaven. Until 5am the next day when hell returned. All this time, Lucy kept me free from other hassles – dealing with the media, promoter, anything and everything else that needed to be looked at, leaving me to concentrate on my training.

The last three weeks before the fight saw me return to

the gym, train at home, stick to Tom's diet and research on Briggs. I watched three fights and began to work out my tactics. He was a jabber. He liked to hit you with three jabs, then hold, looking for a points win. I put the fight together in my head to impose my strengths upon him.

I weighed in at 14 stone two pounds, whilst Briggs was a couple of pounds over the limit. Had it been someone else, I may not have bothered. But because it was Briggs, I insisted he made the weight. Whilst I had a nice relaxing walk in the Peak District, as before the Myers fight, Briggs had the hassle of going for a sauna to squeeze under the weight.

I don't speak to many people on fight day and was happy to be alone with my thoughts. I went back to the hotel for a light meal and a sleep before going into my changing room. It was a long programme of boxing, with me and Briggs being the big one. Lucy shared a moment with me, telling me she knew I would win. For me, this was about putting the past right and winning the cruiserweight title – not just for me, but for Dad.

Once my dressing room was cleared after the pre-fight checks, I was alone with my thoughts. I felt so good, strong, full of energy. Briggs had made the most of my decision to go to the ring last, saying I was buying time before being knocked out. But I knew exactly what I was doing. This was an old trick I learnt as a boy – keep him waiting, wind him up. Even when the music started, I sat in the changing room for another minute or so. A young chap begged me to move, I told him to go away using different words. Then I walked to the ring.

The hotel was packed to the roof. Briggs, being local, had his following but about 80 per cent of the fans were behind me. I have never seen so many T-shirts before with

The Legend on them. Briggs, a Rastafarian, made his ring walk to *Buffalo Soldier*, by Bob Marley and the Wailers, amid a few cheers, then the place went crazy as John Cafferty's *Heart's on Fire,* from the *Rocky* films, signalled my entrance. The announcer told the crowd the title was at stake – no last-minute cop outs this time.

I smiled, allowing the atmosphere to burn into my chest. I was raging inside. I wasn't leaving the ring without my title. Briggs shadow boxed and looked in good shape. "This is my belt, my title ... no way are you getting your hands on it," he said, as the referee gave us the rules. I smiled, turned my back and said nothing. The sheer noise of the crowd drowned out his last verbal shot. I didn't care what he said. The waiting was over and I was ready.

Cornermen Frank and Shaun gave me instructions and words of encouragement, and I knew I had to win well. Briggs was the champion and I've seen so many close fights go either to the home fighter or the one who already holds the title. I had to ensure this one wasn't close to go home with that belt.

Briggs came out like a man possessed. Wild punches flashed well wide of their target as I jabbed and moved, working my opponent out. Then he settled into the routine I knew so well from my research – jab, jab, jab, hold. I knew this was going to be a dirty fight. I backed into the ropes, letting him think I was backing off. Forward he came jab, jab, jab, then, as he was about to hold, I let loose a right hook and left uppercut. I could see he was stunned but didn't change his tactics.

Round two followed the same pattern. I used the ropes and again Briggs walked straight into my punches. I was using all the skills I had learnt over the years to run him ragged, making him run around the ring after me. He was breathing hard, slowly losing energy.

I saw Lucy wave her arms and shout encouragement after round two. I knew I was in front, but I've seen so many good boxers take their eye off the ball in the final rounds and pay the penalty. I told myself to keep going, hang on and work Briggs hard.

Briggs began throwing big punches that missed and I changed tactics briefly to hunt him down, aiming to his body, then switching to the head. I was hitting him hard and it was taking its toll. His legs seemed glued to the floor and he was holding all the time. *Bang!* I got him with a good one and down he went. The referee gave him a standing count. I smiled as he claimed he had slipped and there was no need for the count. His legs told a different story.

The crowd chanted "Wardy, Wardy" before the fourth and final round. His supporters were quiet. Once you've shut the crowd up, it's game over. I saw Briggs blowing like a whale, really struggling. I couldn't wait for the bell. After we touched gloves, I moved forward with a vicious right hook to the side of his head. His legs wobbled, encouraging me to push on. A hook to the body and Briggs was back on the ropes as I let loose.

Best he could do was curl up and grab at me to hold on. I switched tactics and pulled back. This time, and far too late, Briggs walked around the ring, trying to keep his distance. That beckoned me on to attack with a combination of hooks, uppercuts and jabs. When the bell rang, he was exhausted.

It was the longest wait of my life. I'm sure it took an hour for the judges to complete their scorecards and the referee to call us into the centre again. I paced up and down. Lucy was in the ring too. "You've done it, Steve, you beat him," she said. I said nothing. The Smith fight, the politics and all the scheming flashed before me.

Briggs and I embraced and shook hands. We were both wet through with sweat. The referee waited for the announcer to read out the scores then, without me realising I had won, lifted my arm. I was overcome. My head was spinning, my mind blank. I had won the EBF Midlands cruiserweight title! I remember the belt going round my waist, Lucy kissing me and the crowd, including family and mates, chanting "Legend, legend, legend'. There was the flash of cameras and all the sounds. I stood there as a champion. I looked for Mum and Dad for a brief second. I'd done it for them. I had the title Dad so wanted for me.

After what seemed an age, we made our way out of the ring and back to the changing room. My back was bright red, not only from the rope burns but the slaps of congratulations. First to see me was Briggs, with a firm handshake and a few words of congratulations. He was upset, as he would be. I had beaten him and beaten him well. He had lost his title and that takes some getting over. But he showed his respect. He spoke with me about my age and I told him that had nothing to do with it. I had something called heart and now my heart was fully in it, which wasn't the case during my earlier professional career. After time with Lucy, I showered and changed, sitting alone to go through the fight in my mind. The next day, I was going to make a special journey.

Bulwell cemetery was cold and bleak. The trees had lost their leaves, the air was thin. The pale sun failed to warm the ground as I sat alone at Dad's grave with the belt in my hands. There were no tears; I was happy and I know, hand on heart, so was he. I don't remember what I said, but that didn't matter. During those days with Tom, the training and all the shit that had gone with it, I had promised myself this moment – winning, taking the belt to Dad's grave and paying respects to the man who had always been there for me.

The issue of being the oldest boxer in the world and getting into the Guinness Book of World Records was first raised before my title defence against Peter McJob, about 20 years my junior. Lucy looked into the details and the record was held by Australian Dexter 'Dingo' Dunworth, who only taken up the sport at 48 and continued until his mid-50s. It would have been nice to fight him but Dunworth, a nice guy who had worked in a soup kitchen, had hung up his gloves for good.

If you think creating a world record is all about turning up on the day and achieving a remarkable feat, think again. Lucy and I found out there's a hell of a lot more to it. Fortunately Lucy, who is very good at IT, looked after the organisational side of it because it is very time consuming.

The fight was sanctioned by the EBF, both boxers were licensed and we needed to get hold of media reports of the fight. In addition, the referee had to be licensed. Names and numbers of the judges, the master of ceremonies and the cornermen also had to be supplied in advance. They were also strict on the issue of being an active boxer. You had to have fought both over a number of years and been in the ring recently. This safeguards against someone who isn't really a boxer deciding to fight just to create an age record. There were numerous forms to complete and always the worry we might have missed something and the whole event would be invalid.

Even after submitting all the details, there was a 12-week

wait for them to come back to us. Eventually we got the green light about a week before the bout. I was excited about setting the record, but it wouldn't have meant so much to me if I lost my title. I was training with only one thing in mind – to win, not just to take part.

The whiff of a world record in the air ensured a very good turnout at the Escapade Night Club in Chesterfield. McJob made his intentions clear as we stood in the ring waiting for the start. I watched as he made a sign he was going to cut my throat. I didn't respond but turned around to my corner and told them I was going to make him suffer.

The guy was big, muscly and clumsy. He came out very fast, trying to take my head off with every punch. Not only did I make him miss; he even fell over with his wasted effort. I knew that, if he hit me, I could be in trouble because he hit hard. This was always going to be an explosive fight and I needed to get the big punch in first. That's what happened in round two as I put McJob face down on the canvas. When he got up, I clubbed him with a big right hand. It was like a tree being felled. I couldn't see him getting up from that. Somehow, he scrambled to his feet at the count of eight. I was thinking he was a tough bugger and was looking to finish him completely when, like Myers, he got naughty.

It's surprising what people do when they're in trouble, but this shocked me. McJob bit me on my left shoulder. Nobody had ever done that before, not even in my bare-knuckle fights. It was bleeding and I told the referee, but he waved us to fight on. I continued throwing punches until the end of the round, before showing my men in the corner what he had done. The bite made me more determined to finish him as soon as I could. I was hitting him again and knew I was way ahead on points when he tried his next dirty tactic. As the referee was speaking to him, he got me in a headlock. He even tried to physically lift me off my feet.

When the final bell went, I knew I had won and had set a new world record in style. The *Sunday Sport* girls were in the ring and it was mayhem; everyone wanted to talk with me. McJob's first reaction was to say: "Let's finish this outside," and I said I'd be with him in an hour. But he saw sense when he came back into the ring after he changed. "Well done, Steve my man," he said. "I was only joking – you are the best."

I was very proud to be presented with a Champion of Champions achievement belt by John Ashton, and news of what I had done spread far and wide. A little while afterwards I got a phone call from a guy claiming to be George Foreman. My first reaction was that someone was having a laugh, but we started talking and it became clear this really was the great former heavyweight boxing champion.

George had a special interest in my record as he was the oldest-ever world champion. It was a great honour to be personally congratulated by one of the most famous names in the history of the sport – the guy who almost knocked Joe Frazier's head off and was involved in the Rumble in the Jungle, arguably the most famous fight of all time, with my idol Muhammad Ali in Zaire in 1974.

More title defences followed. My next opponent at the Escapade, Keifer Bentley, was particularly dangerous because I knew so little about him, other than that he was from a kickboxing background. It came about because my scheduled opponent, Chad Morby, pulled out at noon on the day of the fight. John told me the bad news after I got to the venue but arranged for another opponent if I was happy to go ahead. With a good crowd guaranteed, I didn't want to let them down.

You might think someone coming in so late is at a big disadvantage but that's only part of the story. I had worked out Morby and how I was going to defeat him. I didn't even know if Bentley was orthodox or a southpaw. I agreed to the switch but got another shock when we got into the ring. Bentley was a seriously big lad. I could have eaten every hat in the house if he was the right weight.

In contrast to my last three fights, this was a proper boxing match. Bentley was strong and this time I got on my bike, stuck out my left hand and moved around. My points win may have been solid rather than spectacular, but I was well pleased to come through. There was plenty on the line in my next outing – a third successful defence would win me the title belt outright. My opponent Lee Renshaw was a big friend and former sparring partner of Briggs. We fought in his hometown of Chesterfield and John warned me about his punching power.

It only took about halfway through the first round for me to discover that for myself as he showed he could give it a bang. Neither of us was taking a backward step. He hit me with some crackers and I gave him plenty back.

I put him down for a count in the second round and he had me in trouble in the third. The moment I hit the deck I was thinking: "This is a 10-8 round." There was no problem getting up and continuing to take the fight to him. I won on points and afterwards Lee was gracious enough to admit that, apart from the knockdown, I had won every round.

What a year that was. The 'old man', who should have been putting his feet up, had defied all odds to fight five times, with five victories, a title win and three successful defences, all against significantly younger opponents. To cap it all, I was officially in the Guinness Book of World Records as the oldest active boxer on the planet.

A couple more fights followed, including a second-round victory in an eliminator for a British title fight when I hit my opponent so hard I broke his ribs, before my run of vintage victories came to an end in unfortunate fashion. It was an English and British cruiserweight fight with a Polish boxer called Arek Drezik.

This was one night when all tactics and pre-fight planning were left in the cupboard because I went hell for leather from the first bell and Drezik was virtually the same. It was a very close six-round fight which a lot of knowledgeable folks thought I just shaded. However, when the judges totted up their scores it was announced as a draw – something that had never happened to me before.

What happened next was even more novel. The promoter Roger Brotherhood, from Mansfield, got us both together and asked us to fight one last round to decide the winner. We both agreed, went toe-to-toe for three more minutes and it was Drezik who won a split decision. It was a tough loss to take and I was desperate for a rematch, but Drezik wasn't interested.

I felt there was more, much more, to come but, then in 2013, I suffered another very unexpected setback. If one horrific accident at work wasn't enough, I suffered another – this time to my right hand. It happened during my first week working for a new company when I was being trained to be put in charge of the concrete mixer.

I was on shift when the training officer discovered a problem – the system was down due to an electrical fault. I asked what he wanted me to do and he said I could hold the bucket in the mixing pod to catch the plasticiser as it dropped down. I said that was fine, if he could show me how to do it.

Then he went across to the panel and pressed the switch, thinking the power was still off. I was hit instantly by 5,000 revs. I managed to get my left hand out of the way but the right one got hit by the blades on the mixer. I had no chance. There was hardly anything left of the bucket and, as for my hand… I've encountered pain in my time but that was something else.

I shouted out and he hit the emergency button straight-away, before running towards me and saying sorry. I told him to get out of my sight. My hand was pounding. The impact split my glove and it was already swelling. I took some deep breaths. This was really hurting. When I went to the toilet, I chewed the rest of the glove off. My hand had swollen big and red, like a boxing glove. Already it was black in places, but strangely there was little blood – almost like a scratch. It was burning but I couldn't stand any cold water on it.

The door opened and the manager and his sidekick appeared. The boss said he understood I'd had "a bit of an accident" and when I showed him my hand, he couldn't believe it. They told me to get myself to Ripley Hospital straight-away. But they were too busy to take me, so I'd have to get there on my own. Yes, you read it right – I needed to drive.

That journey was only six miles, but it was murder. I had to stop a couple of times on the A38 because I was feeling dizzy and sick. I was seen immediately but told my injury was too severe for them to handle – the choice was either Derby or King's Mill. I opted for King's Mill, which was a 12-mile drive and nearer home. That journey was even worse. I had to stop two or three times and tried winding the window down to hold my hand out.

But the wind made it worse and I was again feeling sick. I was taken straight to the triage nurse, then for an X-ray that revealed a series of breaks. My hand was put in a cast and I travelled as planned to see Nigel Benn at a show in Manchester that evening. But, halfway through, I was in such pain that I asked to be brought back home.

I was again feeling claustrophobic in the cast and next day I went back to King's Mill to get my hand put in an elastic covering, which suited me much better. I wasn't very happy with the company's response when I phoned them to say I wouldn't be at work because I needed to go back to hospital. From the start, they seemed to take the attitude the accident was my fault, which I can tell you 100 per cent it wasn't. I was asked to go into work after my hospital visit, so I did.

Seeing my right hand in an elasticated cast, the boss said I shouldn't be driving. I replied that there was no way I should have been driving the previous day either! I almost needed to remind this guy I was as handy with my left hand as my right. At least now they could see with their own eyes I was in no fit state to return to work. The boss was keen to strike a deal. He said that the company would continue to pay my wages on one condition – I didn't take legal action. Although I agreed, I still covered my back by looking into what had happened.

I made some enquiries among my friends at work and found out some very worrying things. The instructor wasn't qualified and automatic knock-off switches had been removed so the machine operated more quickly. I eventually discovered there were seven basic safety procedures that weren't in place. Lucy helped me with getting photographs, documents and witness statements in place in case I needed them.

The procedure was that I called into the office to collect my wages, which were paid in cash. Then, after about six weeks, one of the guys told me to be calm and cool because I might not like what I was going to hear. I had a fair idea where this was heading. Not surprisingly, there was no union man on hand, so I went into the office to talk with the boss alone.

He asked how my hand was and I told him – very truthfully – that it had been put in a different cast and was no better. I was unable to go back into work. He said he was very sorry, but the company was no longer willing to pay my wages. I could have last week's payment, then it would stop. I respectfully reminded him of the promise he had made a few weeks previously and asked if he was willing to pay me. The answer was an adamant no. So, I told him there and then that I would be pursuing a legal claim. He said I had given my word not to do so, but that was on the condition he paid my wages. I left his office telling him the case would kill this place – and I was right.

The solicitor was impressed when she saw all our evidence, describing it as the easiest case he had ever had. She assured me from the beginning that I would win, as the company didn't have a legal leg to stand on. The episode dragged on for about two years from the injury to the final settlement. I continued to go into the office every fortnight or so to update the boss on what was happening and received several financial offers. The boss was desperate to come to an agreement to prevent the case from going to court. "Can we come to a compromise?" he asked.

"In a word, no," I replied. He had chosen the wrong guy

to play with. In the end it went to a court case, and I was approached on the day by a solicitor representing the company with an out-of-court offer. I refused it and told them what I wanted – providing they got back to me very quickly. The solicitor disappeared to make a phone call and returned five minutes later, saying: "You've got what you wanted."

"No," I said. "That was five minutes ago. I told you to be quick." I asked for, and got, three times as much as they originally offered. Justice was done but I was still left with a damaged hand that will never be 100 per cent again. I found out two very disturbing things soon after the case was concluded. Firstly, the company had shut down, but not before another employee had their leg broken in another industrial accident. My fight wasn't only for my benefit but for the sake of others who worked there.

Again, it looked as though my boxing career was all over. But some surprise news soon changed that!

8

MORE WORLD RECORDS AND TITLE DESPAIR

By Lucy Ward

We were both very upset when I discovered an American guy called Mike Palmer had taken Steve's Guinness World Record as the oldest active boxer in the world. The worst thing was that, at that time, there were no guidelines in place to say you had to be a professional boxer for a stipulated period and been active recently. Mike had only had a couple of fights in his career but returned to the ring at the age of 57 to beat Steve's world record.

Our reaction was to get the record back – and now Steve has done that, Guinness have put rules in place to say that the record holder must have boxed over a 40-year span, been active on their 60th birthday and hold a professional licence.

Now we hope Steve will hold the record forever!

W hen Lucy told me she had some 'terrible news', I thought she was going to say someone close had died. That wasn't the case, but Lucy said she knew I'd take this news just as badly. "You've lost your world record!" she said.

Lucy is very on the ball with what is going on and had seen a report online about an American boxer called Mike

Palmer, who had become the oldest active fighter in February 2015 at the age of 57 years 327 days. I was gutted. Totally gutted. Nothing, even a busted hand, was going to stop me from setting the record straight.

I knew I was still physically fit enough to fight and set my mind on a bout with Mike Palmer. That was easier said than done. It was a very difficult task getting hold of Mike's contact details. I looked anywhere and everywhere for a clue. I didn't have a lot to go on as I didn't know either what he did for a full-time job or where he lived. I made endless phone calls and finally got a sniff when I got hold of his works number, a petroleum company.

Not only was this guy a record-breaking boxer, but also a very successful businessman. He was the boss. A woman answered, so I explained who I was and that I was looking for Mike Palmer, the boxer and Guinness world record holder. A couple of minutes later Palmer himself was on the phone. I got to the point and he seemed interested in fighting me. I was keen to bring the fight to Mansfield; he was understandably more interested in keeping it in America.

But first, we needed to get the green light. He was going to look into getting licensed at his end whilst I phoned the President of BIBA, the British Irish Boxing Authority. I was told I would be okay, subject to my annual medical. I organised another visit to Liverpool very quickly and was sitting pretty.

The fight was more in my interests than Mike's, because I'm a year older and therefore would automatically regain the world record by going into the ring with him. But the idea of a battle between the two record holders appealed to him and both of us wanted to win. When I phoned Mike back, he was having problems getting his licence because of his age. I told him I was confident I could arrange for BIBA to licence him if he sorted out his own medical. As arranged, I sent him all the forms to fulfil the medical requirements and things went quiet for a couple of weeks. I was about to ring him again when he phoned. "Steve, I feel so bad," he said. "I have known for a couple of days that I have failed my medical and didn't want to tell you."

He said they had found a shadow on his brain. He even sent me the letter to prove it. I knew he wasn't making excuses. We parted on very good terms, because I knew Mike was genuinely sad about having to quit boxing for good. The whole episode took about a couple of months and left me still scrambling around for an opponent so I could bring the record back home.

I was already in touch with Virgil Hill, a former world light heavyweight and cruiserweight champion who was a friend of Mike's and had planned to be his cornerman. Virgil had returned to the ring again in 2015 after more than seven years and seemed an ideal opponent.

When I suggested that we fight, he said he would have to think about it, but it seemed a good idea. The plan was to fight in America and the onus was on me to come up with the funding. I was paying him to fight me, with support from my sponsors, and came up with a purse which he agreed to. It looked like the fight was on until I took a phone call at three o'clock in the morning. Virgil told me he had been speaking with his new wife and she said he shouldn't be fighting me for the money I had suggested. He then asked for 10 times the amount.

I said I would phone around and get back to him the next day, but my heart wasn't in it. I knew there was no way I could raise the money, even to fight one of the bigger names in the world of boxing. I told him the news when I phoned again and said that I felt a bit let down. Virgil said he was sure we would do business in future and suggested keeping in touch. I didn't do so. He had let me down once; there was no point in going over the same ground again. If it had been me, I would have kept my word.

I was back to square one, but BIBA came to the rescue. Being registered with them, I went through the list of other boxers on their books until I found Jody "One Man Riot" Meikle. Again, there was nobody of my age to fight, so I would be giving away a massive 24 years to this difficult, journeyman boxer from Scunthorpe.

Never in my life have I taken the easy option and chosen an opponent I knew wasn't in my class. With Meikle, I knew hand on heart I was up against it. The fight was held in December 2015 at Shirebook Leisure Centre and lived up to its billing. I gave a good account of myself, but Meikle caught me cold in round three. I dragged myself off the floor a couple of times but there was no coming back. I was beaten fair and square.

It was a major consolation for me that an adjudicator from Guinness World Records, Jack Brockbank, was there to present me with the certificate for regaining the world record. But I genuinely wished I could have won it differently. For the first time in my life, I felt my age in the ring. I knew then that, if I fought again, I needed to find someone of a more similar age.

***

By Tony Delahunty, media personality and managing director of Mansfield 103.2 FM
Commentating on Steve Ward's big fight with Andreas Sidon was something I'll never forget. There was Steve, big monster-cum-

gentle giant and by now a great friend, in the ring with a German giant many years his junior I wouldn't fight with a gun.

Alongside me was Andreas' daughter and the way she spoke, it was like two brothers were in the ring knocking hell out of each other. For some of that evening, I thought Steve was going to beat him. He was on top until a combination of the German's longer reach and younger years turned things around.

If Steve was gutted, he hid it well. He spoke so well about the fans, the occasion and the person who had just beaten him. It was a night for everyone in Mansfield to be proud of. Steve had long since changed my view of boxers. I was known in my office as the journalist who went into the ring with Frank Bruno – it was in a ring above a pub – and I'd always wanted to find out more about them. But Wardy was the last thing I expected when I met him.

I thought boxers would be arrogant, but there's not a hint of that in Steve. There's a simplicity about him, in the best possible sense. And he is a very honourable man in every dealing I have had with him. It was typical of Steve when he invited me and my wife when he was a guest of the female Lord Mayor of Nottingham. I saw there how he charms people.

He knows how to get to the heart of any argument. I wouldn't like to get into a serious row with him, but I'm not sure how that would be possible. Steve is the type who will knock seven bells of shit out of his opponent in the ring, then help him off the floor when the fight is over.

He has been a great mentor to my cricket-playing son Patrick. Steve has taught him boxing skills and fitness to complement his cricket and works him very, very hard. There have been times I wanted to intervene, but Steve gave me a wink or a nod and said: "He'll be okay." Now, he can't wait for that training to resume.

Steve is a terrific human-interest story – one that will probably become bigger and bigger. Apart from being the world's oldest boxer, he is also a bloody good bloke.

***

By Ben Bradley, Mansfield MP
I met Steve Ward whilst he was preparing for his big fight in
Mansfield. I knew he was struggling with an injury but there's a
stubbornness to his character and he was never going to pull out.
He told me this was going to be his last fight and he wanted it to be
in Mansfield. The event was as much for the people of Mansfield
as it was for him and I was impressed by the huge audience he at-
tracted for the fight against Andreas Sidon.
Steve is a recognisable person in the Mansfield area. He is someone
people have seen in their streets and they know him. He is a very
positive and humble person who always wants others to do well.
Steve has a great story to tell and has shown what is possible if you
work hard enough. He is creating his own legacy through his world
records and it is something the whole community can be proud of.

I thought all my dreams were going to come true in July 2017. I planned to bow out of boxing with a world title in front of my home fans in Mansfield – the perfect way to fulfil Dad's prediction. As well as the age issue, I needed to find an opponent with true boxing credentials. I knew straightaway I'd got the right man when I stumbled across German Andreas Sidon.

This guy had a serious boxing record. Winner of 12 out of 13 world title fights, he even knocked out Danny Williams, who beat Mike Tyson, and had fought the giant Russian Nikolai Valuev, dubbed the "Beast from the East." It was a very special occasion for me. Not only was I fighting, but I also arranged and funded the event. The days when I had a manager were long behind me – and I was glad of that.

But it also meant that I did all the donkey work and was worried about the success of the evening as well as taking on one of the boxing challenges of my life. The first task was to try to track Andreas down, which took a few weeks.

Eventually I got him on the phone and immediately he was polite and came across as a really good bloke. I introduced myself and he spoke in broken English. I asked him if he was still fighting and he told me he was. He was happy in principle to come over to England and we agreed that I was funding it. He said he would ring back the next day and was as good as his word. He had given the matter a lot of thought and decided it would be good to fight me.

We set a date and left it to each other to arrange the licensing. I spoke with BIBA and then passed my medical to get mine, but Andreas phoned to say he was having problems because of his age. No problem. I knew I could get him licensed through BIBA if he passed his medical, which he subsequently did.

We agreed on Mansfield Civic Centre as the venue, which was another way I proved the doubters wrong. They said I could never stage a world title fight in the town but doing so meant I was guaranteed great home support. I contacted the World Boxing Confederation who decided to stage it as their first-ever world veterans heavyweight title fight with their president Gene Puckall and the BIBA vice-president Gianluca Di Caro, known as Rio, in attendance. The contest was also sanctioned by BIBA for 12, three-minute rounds.

I needed to arrange backing fights and spoke to Lee Murtagh, who got the national series of boxing lads to fill up the card. Tony Delahunty was to commentate live on *Mansfield Radio*, and *Notts TV* were on board to film it. I was learning a lot about the nuts and bolts of the boxing business away from the ring. I also got Andreas a place to stay whilst in England and arranged for his transport.

I wanted to win the title for Mansfield and knew I could do it. But, after a couple of weeks of full training and during sparring five weeks before the big fight, I suffered a big setback. I went bang, bang, bang with my left hand and then it happened. I couldn't lift my arm up. It felt limp and useless. I had suffered a rotator cuff injury to my left shoulder. What a total nightmare. I had a 20 millimetre and an eight-millimetre tear, and the choice was mine. Pick up the phone to Andreas to tell him the fight was off, or battle on as best as I could. I didn't want to let so many people down. But, as luck would have it, Andreas wasn't well and the fight was put back a month.

That gave me some breathing space as I got my physio Paul Walker on the case. He worked on the injury two or three times a day and it started to ease. I knew I would eventually need an operation but at least I could hit with it – just not very hard. An early operation would have meant no fight, because the medics warned it would take too long to heal. So, I chose to try to heal myself, take the fight and have it operated on afterwards.

I needed to use kidology to ensure the fight went ahead. I should never have passed the medical. After going through the usual bits and bobs, I was asked if I was in any pain. I said no, but the real answer was plenty. Then I was asked to hold my arm up. Best I could do was hold it to the side, but I distracted the person doing the medical, so he didn't see how much I was struggling. All this was a calculated risk on my part and it so nearly came off. Come fight night, I was feeling good. I was confident I was going to win.

Andreas was about five or six years younger and had more experience of fighting over 12 rounds. He was also a big, big man and a more natural heavyweight. It was a case of eat,

eat, eat to build me up to about 15 stones where I felt flabby. The media gave it a good go both locally and nationally and there was a lot of public interest in the fight. Andreas was nothing like some of my recent opponents. We gave each other rightful and mutual respect, both before and after the contest. He was a true professional and this was always going to be a battle.

Sitting in my dressing room about an hour before the fight was different from normal. Usually I go to sleep, getting someone to wake me up about 10 minutes before but, on this occasion, I was going through the arrangements and mentally checking I hadn't forgotten anything. Not ideal preparation for such a big night. *Notts TV* came into my dressing room 15 minutes before the fight for a chat and mentally I was in turmoil, because I still didn't know for certain whether I would be competitive.

The thought went round and round my head, that I was going to let down all the locals who had bought tickets to support me. It was a very special occasion for me and the town of Mansfield, and I had no choice but to refuse to give in to negative thoughts. I decided there and then not to think about my arm again and focus only on the moment.

Then it was time. I was sporting a spangly Union Jack gown and shorts and hooded up to keep the heat in. Being the champion, Andreas chose to enter the ring first. Then it was my turn, surrounded by glamorous ladies Lucy, Anna and Kim and again accompanied by *Heart's on Fire.* The place was going barmy. The atmosphere was second to none, even better than my experience at the Royal Albert Hall.

I listened to the German national anthem for Andreas and felt very patriotic as I stood for *God Save The Queen.* I was doing this for Queen and country, for Mansfield and, of course,

Dad. Just about the only thing missing was Mum and Dad, but I know they were there supporting me in spirit.

I thought I was tall but looked at Andreas and he was a giant. I weighed in at 15 stone two pounds; he was 16 stone seven pounds. My tactics were clear. As Andreas had fought more longer bouts, he was used to slower openings. I decided to make a fast start and try to shake him out of his comfort zone early on.

I caught him with some good shots in round one and there was no doubt the round was mine. As I went back to the corner, my team said: "That's yours, but just watch out for that left hook." I pinned him to the ropes in round two, but his sheer physique got him out of trouble. Nevertheless, I was pleased to get more points on the judges' scorecards.

It was round three when I shook Andreas rigid. I got him in his own corner and was unleashing big shots to the chin. He was all over the place, but then the bell went. Perfect timing for Sidon, and unlucky for me.

The fourth round was lower key but again, I was still forcing the fight and caught him with plenty. Sidon replied with one or two but was largely on the back foot. Every time I went back into the corner, my team were telling me: "You won that round, Steve."

It was the fifth where I again went so close to clinching the title. A left hook, then a right, followed by a combination of punches had Andreas in a bad way. He fell back onto the ropes in his own corner as I continued to bang away. I could see the referee was close to ending the fight in my favour when the bell again came to his rescue. The referee told me afterwards he was one punch away from ending it.

Round six was an opportunity to get our breath back. It was a closer round, but I was still edging it. Then came the turning point of the fight. I caught Sidon with a big left hook but immediately felt pain in my shoulder. It was the first sign of the pre-fight injury coming to haunt me. The shoulder was shaky and wobbly, but it was close to the end of the round and I went back to my corner, knowing that yet again I'd won the round and hoping for the best.

I told my team to get working on my shoulder quick. But Paul, my physio, delivered the verdict: "It's gone completely, Steve." He wanted to pull me out there and then, but I wasn't going to give up when so far in front. I had no choice but to march out for the seventh as if nothing had happened. Perhaps I could throw one big punch and end it before Andreas got to me. I could barely hold my left arm up. Not only was I struggling to throw punches, I wasn't in the best of shape to defend myself.

Sidon sensed blood and caught me with an almighty right to the head. I was down, but not out. I got up at six or seven prepared to carry on. Referee Lee Murtagh looked at me and asked if I was okay, but then stopped the fight. "I know what's happened – that's a rotator cuff," he said. "I know a rotator cuff injury when I see it."

Of course, I was upset. I felt like my whole world had just collapsed in on me. But there was no doubt he did the right thing. The referee's job is to protect the boxers from a potentially serious injury and I was almost an open target. Andreas was in tears. "I didn't win that fight," he said. I was shaken by what had happened to my shoulder and the disappointment of losing when I was so much on top.

I didn't want to talk to anyone. I was feeling sorry for myself. Sitting alone with my thoughts, I wondered if I could have done anything differently. But I couldn't. I fought like a gladiator that night and what happened was beyond my control. That's sport. That's boxing. I congratulated Andreas because it was his night.

I was due to go to work the next day but first visited Andreas in his hotel to ensure all was in order for his return trip home. Once again, Andreas was the perfect gentleman. He admitted he was all-but beaten in the third and fifth rounds, and barely knew where he was when the bell sounded. He presented me with two of his world title belts – a white leather belt WBU and a brown leather belt for the WBB. I accepted them because it was a really nice thing to do.

But I couldn't parade them as my own because they belonged to him rather than me. I later had them marked as "Andreas Sidon, champion and Steve Ward, challenger" because that was the truth. Andreas also said something very special. "A week before I came here, my brother died. Now you are my brother – and a real champion."

The judges presented me with the official scorecards afterwards – I was seven points in front on all three scorecards. That meant I won six rounds, including one by a two-point margin. I was gutted rather than bitter, though, because I know it was an honest fight and Andreas was a worthy champion. I didn't consider myself a loser because I gave it my all. I'm sure the fans who supported me at ringside would agree that I gave them plenty to shout about. I feel pride because we put together a very special night for the people of Mansfield who have always been so good to me.

In my opinion, you could have called me a loser had I chosen a far easier opponent and ducked out of boxing with an easy win. That would have looked good in the history books but wouldn't have satisfied me or won me a world title. I've kept in touch with Andreas since the fight and a couple of years ago Lucy and I even went to Germany to celebrate the New Year with him and his family. That's the true spirit of boxing. I have the utmost respect for any boxer who goes into the ring and puts his body on the line, and I'll always have time for Andreas and treasure taking part in a very special night.

As I was writing this book, Andreas got in touch with me and suggested a rematch in England. For the best possible reasons, I have let the matter lie. I don't want to go into detail, but I saw things when we visited Andreas that made me worry for him. He is talking about an exhibition bout, but I don't think he could pass a medical. I know, however, he will have been cheering me on in 2021 and I wish him and his family well in their future.

My rotator cuff injury was operated on a week after the fight. I didn't dare tell the consultant what I had been doing after the last time I had seen him. My version of rest was to take part in a world heavyweight title fight. The game was given away, though, by a couple of people in the hospital shouting: "Hey up, champ ... we saw the fight."

The medics told me it wouldn't get much better despite the operation. I was finished and should never take part in boxing again. They advised that I would never be able to lift a weight again above my head and I would never be able to use my left arm to punch again, as it could rip totally off the bone. But I wasn't having that. I adapted my exercise routine in my training and had the will to make it happen. Today it's not perfect. But much, much better.

9

THE LONELIEST PLACE ON EARTH

By Michael Wildgust, Lord Mayor of Nottingham, 2011
Steve Ward is a brilliant advertisement for Nottingham and
Nottinghamshire. I invited him to a reception at the Council
House in Nottingham during my year as Lord Mayor, having
read about his feats in boxing and seen him on TV.
His achievements in the ring have been fantastic, particularly
for someone of his age. Speaking with him again in 2021, he told
me he was still boxing and was going to beat his next opponent.
Steve is a man of determination and his heart is in it, age doesn't
matter.
I think he has now finally hung his gloves up – although he would
probably box on until he was 90, if he was allowed. It's great for
the area that we have a Guinness Book of World Records holder.
Now he deserves official recognition for what he has done over
the years.

"Why do you do it? Why put your health at risk at your age?"

If only I had a tenner for every time someone has made remarks like that to me. They don't really know me, do they? I have the ultimate respect for anyone who goes into a boxing ring, whether a world champion or a journeyman struggling to make a living. Because the boxing ring really is the loneliest place on earth. Whether it's Madison Square Garden in New York, with half the world watching, or a small working men's club, it doesn't matter.

My first answer to those who question me is: "Why not?" Age is just a number; I've kept myself very physically fit all my life and know my body and my business inside out. I go through the same medical tests as any professional boxer in Liverpool every year and come through with flying colours. I am told I have the body of a man in his twenties, despite the serious injuries I have suffered.

But the real answer is that I box because I love it. I think about what I will do when I hang up my gloves for good and sometimes it frightens me. And I'm not joking. In life, you can sometimes fool yourself – tell yourself you have done something when you haven't. When you approach the boxing ring, there's no hiding place. You've either put in the hard work or you haven't. Inside that ring, you come face-to-face with the truth.

I love training and I train very hard. It certainly draws a reaction from locals when they see me out on the streets pounding away on my bicycle or running up hills backwards. My training is a big part of my general health as well as my fitness. When younger boxers see me in the gym, they sometimes stare at me and wonder what I am up to. I have redesigned some of the exercises to suit my own body. I do press-ups where I hold myself in position for up to a minute instead of the usual movements. One lad asked why I did that and I told him I was exercising much more of my body, but I would recommend he was very careful if he tried to repeat it. After a few seconds, this young fighter, probably 40-odd years younger than me, said it was impossible.

I know my body and what it is capable of. That's part of the secret. I push it to its limits, but I know how far it can go. It's through exercise, as well as medical treatment, that I have overcome horrific injuries to my foot, my hand and shoulder. I've been told by the top specialists in the land that I would only recover so far – I'd never be able to walk properly or lift my arm to punch again. But I've proved them wrong because I know myself and there's that 'something' inside me that makes me a champion.

I don't need anyone else – trainer or manager – to hold my hand. People watch me and tell me I'm crazy. That there's something wrong with me. But that's me. I enjoy it and I can do it. I've done it in the past and I'm still doing it today. Apart from the treatment I have received for the accidents, I can't remember the last time I went to my GP because of my health. I honestly can't remember. I've seen so many of my friends let themselves go and it's heartbreaking. Some are no longer with us; others aren't in the best of health.

But we all need a goal – something to aim for at the end of all that effort. That makes all the sacrifice worthwhile. Without the fight, I'd only be ticking over; not being satisfied. Yes, I've trained and mentored other boxers. I enjoy it and I'll continue to do it. But does it give me as much satisfaction as getting into the ring myself? No. Being a trainer or a manager after I finish boxing isn't for me. It can never replace the real thing.

Lucy will tell you I start to change in the last couple of weeks before the fight. And she doesn't like it. She says I become a different person – difficult to talk to and be with. And that's putting it mildly. I'm beginning a process they call "going into the zone". All my focus is on the fight. Nothing and nobody else comes close. The zone is like a form of self-hypnosis. It's not easy to explain but, having been hypnotised, I know that's true. That was at a show by well-known professional entertainer Ken Webster in Blackpool. Dared to go forward by my mates, my mind was taken over and I did strange things such as disco dancing – really not my thing – and, thinking I knew everything about a perfect stranger, telling him his wife was a nymphomaniac! It was exciting and scary at the same time. Like the person I become on fight day.

Some people like to psyche themselves up. I don't need that. When I get into the dressing room, I like a nap. I save my physical and emotional energy by going to sleep and then being woken up about an hour before. It's when I'm getting my gloves on and my hands taped that I begin to slip into a deeper focus. I don't want to know anyone or anything, just be alone with my thoughts. There's a job to do and I'm going to do it.

I've told you the story of our wedding. Yes, I wanted to get married – I wanted it very much. But I told Lucy I was preparing for a fight and couldn't let anything else get in the way. Most people say they are nervous on their big day – I was totally relaxed. Getting married was a walk in the park compared with going into that ring.

The forfeits begin when you're young. "Sorry I can't go out, I'm training!" I would have loved a night out with my mates, but I really, really couldn't. I needed to be true to myself when I got in that ring. In later life, everything gets put on hold, from going out for a meal to booking holidays. Lucy will tell you how hard it is. The preparation must be right.

I like the showbiz that goes with boxing. I love the entrance music, the razzmatazz and being walked down to the ring by the girls – particularly my beautiful Lucy. But do you know something? I'm not there. Not in my head. I don't hear the music nor see the people. I'm alone in my own world, conflicting thoughts running through my head. In one ear come the doubts. Have you trained hard enough? Are you fit enough? Have you got a headache? I shoot these down one by one. I tell myself: "This is my time. I'm going to win. Tonight's my night."

Being focused makes the next bit easier. There are four steps up to that ring – climbing those steps is difficult. Too difficult for some. I've known fighters literally take two steps forward and two steps back. Focus is the best solution. I'll tell you a story from my amateur boxing days. I was an experienced boxer by this time and asked to do a young guy a favour. His name was John and he was 12. I recognised that look of fear in his eyes as he approached the ring. He climbed the first two steps and said: "I don't feel very well." That was fear talking. "Do what you do every day," I told him, referring to the hard work he put in training and sparring.

As soon as he was in the ring, John was as sick as a pig. Without any fuss, I got a mop and bucket and mopped it up. With still no sign of his opponent, I got him to sit in the corner with his arms and legs down and breathe. I was getting him anchored; calming him down. When his opponent got into the ring, John asked what I knew about him. Absolutely nothing, I replied, but I'd overheard the very bad things he had said about John's sister, who was on the front row. He asked if I was telling the truth. "Would I lie to you?" I replied.

"I will kill him," said John, suddenly focused.

"I just thought you ought to know," I said. Now he was in

a different world. When they touched gloves in the middle of the ring, I heard John call him a bastard before he walked back to his corner and looked at his dad. He couldn't wait for the bell to go. The two boxers were about the same size, but John was all over him from the start. The contest was over inside the first round as the referee intervened to stop John's opponent taking further punishment. The other kid never stood a chance.

Back in the corner, John said: "He will never say anything about my sister again."

"He never said anything about your sister in the first place," I confessed.

"So, you lied to me?" he replied.

"Never trust anyone!" I said. John was in his own world that day. I make sure I'm in mine.

The crowd may be making a racket – they might be all for me or all against me, but honestly it makes no difference. The only time I remember the shouts of the crowd was the first fight I had back as a professional after meeting Lucy. She was at the front and she and her mates made themselves heard, big time. But that's rare – very rare.

I'm never nervous. That's been my state of mind through-out my career. As far as worrying is concerned, I always let my opponent suffer rather than me. Going into a fight nerve-free is the equivalent of being 140 per cent fit. Nerves can take away from your fitness. I've seen fighters who spar and train particularly well but freeze as soon as they get into the ring. When you are nervous, it can slow down your physical movements and also means you don't think quickly or clearly enough.

Usually, I'm last into the ring. That's the way I like it. Keep my opponent waiting a little longer; play on his nerves. The announcements are made and I barely hear them. I raise my hand in the air to acknowledge my name and that's it. The referee goes about his business. I know the routine off by heart. "No low blows," ... "When there's a knockdown, go to the neutral corner," ... "When I say break, break,' and all the rest. I nod, but I'm not listening. I'm telling myself over and over that I'm going to win. I don't pay much attention to my opponent. Sometimes he will try a mind game, maybe flicking his head at me as we stand there. I don't react; just stare. Keep the focus.

Now back in my corner, I've got three men working with me. I know to my cost in the past that these must be right. A cornerman can win you or lose you the fight. One is more important than the others for me. That's the one inside the ring. His is the only voice I listen to. I don't want the others barking instructions. I want things nice and clear. This man is my extra pair of eyes and ears – and I need him to be knowledgeable. He must know me and my technique; must know boxing and have done it in the ring. A man who has had a few hours on the punchbag is no use to me. I know instantly whether he is giving me good advice or not.

I sit back in my corner with my legs out and arms by my side – never pent-up. That is to prevent the build-up of lactic acid. That way, my body won't tighten up and my energies will flow. In those few seconds, I'm thinking about making a fast start. I never hang about. Get in there, get on top, win the first round. If I win round one, that's one more he must win before he has a chance.

During those three minutes, the only voice I listen to is the referee. He will make himself heard and control the fight. The battle itself can be brutal and hard, but it's also a game of chess. That's something for intellectuals, but boxing needs a different kind of sharpness. I need to anticipate his next move and try to manoeuvre my opponent into a vulnerable position. That's chess, but with more riding on it than pride. In boxing, you are looking after your life.

One thing I've learnt more and more over the years is that it is just as important to avoid the punches as giving them. There's one thing a boxer can't do anything about. Can't train for. You either have a good chin, or you haven't. There aren't the muscles there to build up. When you see a punch, you duck out of harm's way. The big punch is the one you don't see. But there's a secret to taking one on the chin and that's your legs. The punch goes down from your chin to your legs. That's where the right training comes in.

Arnold Schwarzenegger may have good muscles, but does he have good muscles on the back and the front of his legs? For a boxer, they need to be balanced. That's why I run backwards up hills. It evens out the muscles.

Sometimes the big punch hurts like hell; sometimes it's absorbed by riding it or by shock. When Andreas Sidon hit me a good, clean blow to my temple when I could barely raise my arm to defend myself in our world title fight, I went down but didn't feel it. It disorientated me more than anything. But I made a mistake – a very human mistake. Our initial response to being knocked down is to get up. Straight back up. Instead, you should stay down – take an eight count, allow the head to clear.

I'll give you another 'secret' to my longevity in boxing – sheer good fortune! I was at a posh Christmas do in Nottingham when introduced to a woman called Carole. We talked for about five minutes or so and she took some convincing that I boxed. She couldn't see any of the twitching, puffed up eyes, or other physical signs of being a boxer.

I told her the reason was because I am lucky. Yes, lucky! Alongside the ringcraft and knowledge I have picked up over the years, I've had the sheer good fortune to stay clear of the worst punishment. Yes, I lost a lot of my professional fights, and the bare-knuckle stuff is brutal, but someone must have been on my side because the worst injuries I have received in life have always been outside the ring. I've seen enough stars in my time to know they exist. I've broken countless bones but always been well enough to fight on.

Another 'secret' is broken bones can be healed; a shadow on the brain is another thing altogether. I welcome the scanners they have today as a modern miracle. They can help prevent some of the brain injuries caused in boxing. It is a subject I am very clued up on and realise is very important. I did a course to find out more and I know the signs.

I can pick it up in speech and another sign is the eyes. I was at a boxing show about four years ago when a boxer I knew quite well, called Andy, was taking a lot of punishment. I stood up from my seat and shouted: "Stop the fight!" That wasn't enough, they weren't taking any notice, so I shouted: "Stop the f****** fight!" Using the language was the only way I could get the message through.

The referee stopped the fight and I spoke with Andy. I asked if he was alright and studied his response. The right words came out – eventually – but I could tell he was suffering. His eyes were very dilated. I told the people around him to get him to hospital straightaway. He was kept in for observation and was fine, I'm glad to say. But I've seen the opposite. I don't want to name names but one of the boxers I beat was showing signs of brain damage. Real signs. And, yes, it is a hazard of boxing. Hopefully, the scans can help to limit the damage in future before it gets out of hand.

Winning means trying to beat your opponent to a pulp. But, once the fight is stopped or the final bell sounds, that all changes. When I've won, my first thought is to make sure my opponent is okay. The last thing I want is for him to suffer any permanent damage. This is when I start to hear the roar of the crowd. It's like the volume being switched up on the TV. The focus begins to drift and normal life floods in – bit by bit.

The feeling of elation takes over. That numbs some of the pain from the fight. Rather than feeling tired, I may go out to party. It's next morning before reality sets in when I can barely move my hand. I'll go and see the lads in the gym and talk about the fight. I'll have four or five days off. Then it's back into training – a two or three-mile run, 30 minutes or so on the punchbag and pads.

Only a fellow boxer really knows what you go through. I'm very, very thankful for all the support I've had from friends and people from Mansfield and Nottingham but the opinions I treasure are from the fighters. That's why I was so proud when George Foreman, one of the great world heavyweight champions, phoned to congratulate me on one of my world records. As the oldest heavyweight champion in history at the age of 46, he knew more than anyone what it takes not only to be the best, but to continue to box years after most have given up.

Hearing his words filled me with almost as much pride as looking at the list of the world's oldest boxers. Aside from George, there's Archie Moore, Roberto Duran and Larry Holmes, another great I have had personal contact with. I met Larry Holmes and heard him talk about one of his biggest regrets. It drove him to tears to give the man he idolised and used to spar with, Muhammad Ali, the beating of his life.

It takes far more than luck and determination to box on years after most have hung up their gloves. Boxers continue longer in the tooth than fighters. We have learnt one of the most important lessons of all: pugilism is all about hitting without being hit. And there's one 'Steve Ward, from Mansfield' at the top of them all. Do you know how that makes me feel? I can imagine Dad being with me now. I know that in later life I have done him proud.

The bare-knuckle fighting probably helped. If I'd known fully what I was getting into, I wouldn't have done it. I wouldn't recommend it to anyone. The horror of what I saw and experienced will live with me forever. I broke more bones than I knew I had. But all experiences in life can teach you a lesson if you are willing to learn. And I learnt that only 100 per cent will do.

In my amateur career, boxing was a sport. As a professional, it became a business. In bare-knuckle, you are fighting for your life. It's you or him – so it must be you. I came through knowing more hospitals than ever before, but unbeaten and alive. I learnt the hardest way possible what it takes to be a champion.

When the skills of that amazing Chinese surgeon and my bloody mindedness and determination pulled me through my serious foot injury, I knew I had something more to offer. I wasn't going to sit on the sofa and enjoy the easy life. I promised friends that if I could have the gift of walking again, I would go back and do what I do best – box!

I still had ambitions to fulfil. After picking up a multitude of prizes as an amateur, a belt and a title eluded me as a pro. How I ached to take that Midlands cruiserweight title off Dennis Sheehan. When that was denied me, it left a hole in my life. Then, in my fifties, it all came together. Suddenly this was my time and I've loved every minute of it.

Getting myself into the Guinness Book of World Records was the furthest thing from my mind. But when Lucy, my wife, my lover, my inspiration from the time I was so lucky to meet her, told me all about it, I wanted to know. Many people probably think it's a daft record. I know differently. Guinness take the record of the world's oldest boxer very seriously. They guard against it being held by a pretender. It is literally the oldest active boxer and they go to great lengths to ensure the boxing is real.

If I'm the oldest, I have no doubt who was the greatest. Muhammad Ali was my hero. The one I loved and rated above all others. He made the sport of boxing into a work of art. His dancing feet and lightning-quick hands enabled him to pull off the near miracle of winning the world heavy-weight title back at the age of 34 against Foreman. Yet the Parkinson's that tormented him during his final years was surely related to the punishment he took in the ring. He couldn't do what all his fans wished for him – go out at the top.

In Ali's case and that of others who finally paid the price, it wasn't the number of fights that nailed them, but the na-ture of them. A boxer who has fought 40 times and got the job done nice and early may take less punishment than one who has only been in the ring on 20 occasions but been involved in brutal battles going the distance.

Who will ever forget Ali's three fights with Joe Frazier, another of my favourite heavyweights? I can only imagine the toll those incredible battles took on both. Joe's speech was beginning to slur before he finished; Ali finished as a punch bag for Holmes.

I have a quote from my idol in my lounge at home: "Champions aren't made in a gym. Champions are made from something deep inside them." It's brilliant, and so true! Trainers and managers don't 'make' champions. Trainers have a part to play in influencing a champion to fulfil their potential but even they can't put that certain something inside you if it's not there in the first place. Managers do very little in my experience – apart from line their own pockets. They tend to think about themselves rather than their boxers.

Ali had that 'something'. Millions of us throughout the world saw it. When we listened to Ali, we knew he was special, nothing like a run-of-the-mill fighter. Call him arrogant, if you wish. But that 'arrogance' was backed by what he could do in the ring. Ali was in his prime as Cassius Clay before he was banned from boxing for three years. He was the undefeated heavyweight champion of the world and, although everyone wanted his crown, few got near it. Our own Henry Cooper, bless him, went as close as anyone.

His opponents claimed to be unaffected by the way he spoke – but I saw it in their eyes. As they were walking into a ring, I saw a different look to when they were fighting other boxers. Clay had them beaten before they even fought him. They were beaten psychologically.

After he returned as Muhammad Ali, Joe Frazier broke the spell and he had to dig deeper. His victory over George Foreman in Zaire, where he regained the title was incredible. The punishment he took that night was incredible. He was clobbered and clobbered, by maybe the most powerful puncher on the planet, again and again, before his 'rope-a-dope' tactics paid off and he got his man. I don't think for one moment Ali would have agreed to fight George a second time.

The deterioration in Ali in his last few fights was obvious for us all to see. It happens to almost all boxers, unless they get out at the very top, and it happened to the greatest of them all. You could see in his movements; he wasn't the same man. He no longer had the dancing feet and reflexes to avoid the punishment handed out by younger fighters.

Did Ali need the money? I don't know. But he ended his career by losing fights he shouldn't have lost, which was sad. It may seem strange for a boxer of 65 to say Ali went on too long, but I know all about the signs of deterioration. The keys are how long it takes you to prepare and how long it takes to recover. When I was a young amateur, I was involved in some brutal fights but an hour or two later I felt like I hadn't been in a fight at all. More recently, it takes me a day or so to recover.

I do though counter my age with the way I think. I take the words of Lee Li very seriously. He told me age is unimportant. It is not how many years you have been here that counts in your mind, or even how old you feel, but how old you want to be. If I went into the ring thinking I'm a man of 65, I'd be collecting my old age pension before I knew it. I'd fight like a man of 65 and look a fool. Instead, I tell myself I'm a man of 30 and I train and fight that way.

I never met Ali, but I did come face to face in the ring with my second idol, "Marvellous" Marvin Hagler. It happened through the man who was managing me at the time, who rang and asked if I was fit and would spar in London for £70. When he told me it was with Marvin Hagler, I was thrilled. The American was over here to fight Alan Minter and meeting him was surreal. Better than that, I was going to be in the same ring!

Hagler was the ultimate warrior, and here he was with Steve Ward. I was told we would have four rounds of "light, fast sparring" and I wasn't nervous. We came out from the first bell and it was fast sparring. Hagler was a southpaw, which is always awkward, but I genuinely caught him in round two. It was the classic way of combatting a southpaw – right hand, left hook combination. To make it tougher for Hagler, he was coming onto my punch rather than moving away. He knew he had been hit and it shook him, believe me. Obviously sparring is different from a fight. You must temper your aggression and not follow up when your opponent is hurt. The bell went and I said to my cornerman: "That seemed like a short three minutes."

"Yes," he said. "It was just over two!"

The next two rounds seemed more like two hours and three minutes. To put it bluntly, Hagler knocked the shit out of me. He was holding back a touch but still punching me from every angle. It was like there was a third person in the ring, punching me on the sly. I couldn't get near him again. He was good; bloody good. Very fast and elusive. Afterwards I apologised for catching him with the hook, but he said: "No, that's the game. But I'll tell you something. You don't have to go to war all the time. Save your wars for the ring when you get paid for it."

He didn't say it to have a go but taught me something that day. You must be careful. Say you are sparring with three people in a day; that could be three 'wars' and that's a lot of blows to the head and the body. Hagler was shaken because of his own mistake. Had he moved away, he would have taken the sting out of it. Hagler added that sparring was all about showing your ringcraft and speed.

I found him a nice genuine guy and left London with no doubt he would beat Minter, even though Minter was a fantastic fighter. He did. You don't get the nickname "Marvellous" for nothing. I enjoyed watching Hagler box against fellow greats Roberto Duran, Sugar Ray Leonard, Thomas 'The Hitman" Hearns and my own stablemate Tony Sibson, who gave him a contest.

Hagler was clever. He tired out rather than flattened opponents. He never threw five punches when he could throw six. It was his continual onslaught that wore down his man. He hit a lot on the arms when his opponent had a high guard. Instead of trying to push the guard down, he was weakening the arms until he had a bigger target.

I also met Marvin Hagler through work and social occasions which confirmed my high opinion of him. A few years after the sparring session, I got a call from John Ashton asking me a favour. He needed a couple of people to shadow Hagler at a question-and-answer session. I can't remember whether it was in Birmingham or Manchester, but I was excited at the opportunity and my fellow doorman Brian Proverbs was more than happy to have a night off at The Banque to come with me. That night I felt on top of the world. I kept looking at Hagler and he looked back at me. A few words were exchanged but I'm not sure he recognised me.

The next occasion was eight years ago when my friend Tony Marshall invited me to a posh do Hagler was hosting in Sheffield. We listened to the great man speak, then joined the long queue for autographs. When we get to the front, he was sat there with his wife Kay beside him. "How are you, Marvin?" I said. He looked at me and asked if we had met. He still couldn't place me as a boxer until I reminded him of the time nobody in the UK wanted to spar with him. "The man with the big left hook," he said, shaking my hand. "So nice to see you!" He held up the queue whilst he spoke with me, then invited me back a few minutes later.

Hagler asked if I was still boxing, and said: 'Wow' when I told him I was fighting against people decades younger. He even called me "Marvellous Steve Ward."

"That's okay, mate," I said. "The Legend will do."

Joking aside, Marvin Hagler was a down-to-earth, likeable guy and his wife was the same. He wasn't up himself because of what he achieved in the ring. I was totally gutted when I heard in March 2021 that he had passed away suddenly at the age of 66. It hurt me a great deal for that to happen, and I sent my condolences straightaway to his family. RIP, "Marvellous" Marvin Hagler.

***

Boxers are best qualified to talk about the sport. TV watchers and fellow fans have all got their views. But unless they have been in a ring, they honestly have no idea. At a talk I was giving to a Rotary Club, one gentleman bugged me by continually interrupting with his version. Eventually I'd had enough and asked him straight if he had ever been in a boxing ring. The answer was no. Had he ever tried to climb those steps to get into a ring? No. How does it feel to climb those steps? He didn't know.

Then I gave him a very good tip – allow his brain to click in and let his mouth go to sleep for a while. They say you play cricket, play football or play tennis – they never 'play' at boxing. It's a serious sport and everyone who gets into that ring has my respect. In fact, they're all champions in my eyes.

Boxing should be about two fighters getting in the ring and doing the business. Everyone interested in the sport knows it, but managers too often exploit the public and ruin their entertainment. To be honest, their main mission is filling their own pockets rather than benefitting their fighters and the fans.

So, for years we have seen Britain's two heavyweight greats, Anthony Joshua and Tyson Fury, kept apart. At the time of writing, there's more talk of a two-fight deal. I don't know which is worse, not fighting at all or having two fights. Put it this way, I would not pay money to watch a return fight unless the first one was very close. If fight one is won by four or five points or a knockout, why ask the public to lash out more cash – and tickets are very expensive – to watch it happen all over again? That's why there was little public stomach for a third fight between Fury and Deontay Wilder.

A lot of matches at a high level are fixed up these days with a second fight as an option. Sometimes it can work as insurance policy for the higher-ranked fighter with more to lose. It certainly did for Joshua after he was beaten for the first time in his professional career by Andy Ruiz. The guarantee of a rematch meant Joshua was able to pick himself off the floor after a poor performance and get back on track with a unanimous points decision.

Let's hope we do eventually see Joshua and Fury in the same ring for the sake of all British boxing enthusiasts. And as for how I rank on top of some great names in the history of boxing, courtesy of the *Oldest.org* website, here are the 10 oldest professional boxers in the world...

10: Antonio Tarver, USA (Oldest while still active: 47)
9: Archie Moore, USA (47)
8: George Foreman, USA (48)
7: Roberto Durán, Panama (50)
6: Bob Fitzsimmons, England (51)
5: Bernard Hopkins, USA (51)
4: Dewey Bozella, USA (52)
3: Larry Holmes, USA (52)
2: Jack Johnson, USA (60)
1: Steve Ward, England (64)

THE DREAM FIGHT THAT NEVER WAS

By Jimmy 'Hawk' Lloyd, founder of the Universal Boxing Alliance

Having founded my own boxing board, the UBA, in 2016 and still boxing semi-professionally, I was contacted by Charles Russo online. I was impressed with what he told me about his organisation, the Boxing and Mixed Martial Arts Fighters' Union, and his views on supporting the rights of boxers. I've staged about 15 live shows but thought it was a good idea to work with Russo as the BMMAFU appeared to be a bigger organisation.

The fight with Steve came about when Russo phoned to say he was looking for an opponent aged at least 50 for Steve Ward. I am now 55 and was happy to take part in what sounded like a very exciting show – Boxing at Sea. I didn't even want paying because taking part would be particularly good for the UBA and my boxers.

I must admit I had never heard of Steve. But, looking him up, I found out what a star he is – still boxing at 64 and the holder of three Guinness World Records. I was very much looking forward to fighting and meeting him. When we spoke on the phone, I said that, after the fight was done, we'd become friends on the cruise. My suspicions that all was not right started before Boxing News publicised the story. Charles promised a pair of boxing gloves and a belt from a fight involving Billy Joe Saunders. They never came. There were also odd things such as Charles suddenly asking for money for my visa to the Bahamas when I knew it was free. The article then opened my eyes a lot further. I realised then that a lot of us – me and Steve included – had been taken for a ride. I would have realised a lot earlier, but the Covid-19 pandemic was the perfect cover. All UBA events have been cancelled since the end of 2019 so when Charles' shows were postponed, I didn't think much of it. I did get more sceptical though when I suggested events could be staged on pay-per-view and he didn't give me a proper answer.

I'm upset because now I believe Charles Russo is a conman and a liar. I don't think he has ever put on a boxing show and never will. Now I've joined the growing number of people he has blocked. The only consolation is that I told my followers not to send any money in advance and I did the same.

As things have turned out, I couldn't have fought anyway because I have since found out about an eye injury that means I now must retire. The one good thing is that I have now met Steve Ward and I hope that we can work together in the future. He is a great guy and I respect him very much.

***

By Oliver Fennell, Boxing News

I interviewed Steve Ward for Boxing News *magazine in August 2020, as part of a wider story on the sport's minor championships. Boxing's big leagues are represented by the 'big four' – the WBC, WBA, IBF and WBO – but there are a range of other championships, of varying degrees of prestige.*

Steve fought for one such belt, the World Boxing Confederation, when he was 60 years and 10 months old. This made him not only the world's oldest professional boxer, but also the oldest boxer to contest a championship. It was an absorbing angle as I explored the quirks and characters of the minor championship scene, yet

Steve's existing accomplishments were not even the most interesting part of his story. He was plotting the perfect finale to his remarkable career, by fighting again and breaking his own record just four months shy of 65, for another title, and an event that promised to make history for reasons beyond his own Guinness-ratified participation.

Steve Ward vs Jimmy Lloyd was to headline the first night of a groundbreaking fight festival called Boxing at Sea – the world's first boxing promotion staged on a cruise, with a vessel departing from Miami in May 2021 bound for the Bahamas and treating fans to not only three consecutive fight nights while riding the high seas, but also a chance to mingle with legends of the sport on board and a roster of other entertainers.

It was a brilliant idea and Boxing News *was keen for me to cover it. A work trip to Florida and the Caribbean to cover boxing and hang out with the likes of Riddick Bowe and Mia St John? Sign me up! Steve told me to get in touch with Charles Russo, who was not only the organiser of Boxing at Sea but also the president of the BMMAFU. The cruise event in itself was fascinating but the fact that Russo had also established a badly-needed union for combat sports was well worth a story too.*

I interviewed Russo and he came across as ebullient, gregarious and charismatic. His union was exactly what boxing needed and he sounded like a force for good, helping house and employ vulnerable ex-boxers as well as safely guiding active pros through the myriad legal hazards of their occupation. He also provided free health insurance to competitors in this, the most dangerous of sports. He was also absolutely enthused by the prospect of Boxing News *covering his cruise event and said he'd put me up in a cabin on board, plus a night in Miami either side, with full journalistic access to the glamorous names involved.*

Alas, if Boxing at Sea and a combat sports union sounded too good to be true, that's because it was precisely that. As Steve would also find out in due course, Russo's world appears to have been an elaborate scam, albeit a highly convincing one, seemingly ripping off the very same athletes his union claimed to protect. I don't believe there is such a boxing union or ever will be Boxing at Sea. In fact, I don't believe there has ever been and never will be any boxing shows organised by Charles Russo, because even that very identity appears to be false.

After Boxing News *published my interview with him, numerous people got in touch to level some very serious accusations against Russo. Mortified that I may have given a 'conman' a platform of authenticity, and with the full backing of my editor, I embarked on a months-long investigation into Russo and his BMMAFU. I learned that everything his critics said was true, and everything he said was false. He appears to have scammed dozens, if not hundreds, of people, with Steve being just one of them. And, as Steve himself will tell you, the lost money is not the worst of it – it's the deliberate dashing of dreams that is perhaps most immoral. Steve, like many others before and since, had his hopes raised just so another man could line his pockets.*

I have come across some very corrupt people in the boxing world but Charles Russo, in my opinion, could give most of them lessons. The following is a horror story of how my world collapsed at the end of March 2021, just six weeks before I thought I was going to fulfil my lifelong ambition. I shouldn't have believed a word Russo told me. The reason I did was probably because he claimed to be offering exactly what I wanted. My whole life seemed to have led me to the point where I would finally make Dad's prediction about me being a world boxing champion come true.

It all began with a phone call shortly after the start of lockdown in 2020 from my friend, Lee Murtagh. Lee was the referee of my last fight in July 2017 and said he had something I might be interested in. He was to be head referee at a show hosted by a guy he described as a "major player" and a "very, very wealthy American." He was referring, of course, to Russo.

The show was called Boxing at Sea and was history-making, because it would be the first time the sport had been staged on water. The venue was a moving cruise ship bound for the Bahamas. Lee said Russo already had a lot of financial backing for the event and may well be interested in me. He suggested I had a think, then let him know if I wanted him to put me in touch.

There was little need for thinking time – I was immediately sold on the idea. Boxing is still my biggest love in life and this was my chance to get back into the ring at the age of 64 and create a fourth Guinness World Record. I like to do my own research and come to my own conclusions. So, I looked at Russo. I found out he did long podcasts and liked what he was saying. He had founded his own board, the Boxers and Mixed Martial Arts Fighters' Union, and said his mission was to put the interests of boxers first, ahead of managers, promoters and the business side of a corrupt sport. His boxing board also helped fighters and former fighters who were down on their luck with accommodation and other practical issues. This sounded like music to my ears after what I had experienced.

I phoned Lee back the next day saying that, if he had no reason to doubt Russo, I wanted to talk with him and get on board. It struck me as slightly strange when Lee said Russo was mostly contactable on Facebook. I wasn't on that form of social media and had no intention of being so, but Lee told me that this was my best chance of getting an audience with a very busy man. He was apparently a very successful businessman, who had made his fortune in real estate in the United States and other parts of the world, and reluctant to risk wasting time talking to people he didn't recognise.

I tried for about two months to get hold of Russo. I joined Facebook, rang him and left many messages. I heard nothing back and was getting nowhere. I was on the point of giving up completely, but Lee encouraged me – he had spoken with Russo and he was indeed interested in working with me.

He said Russo had joined forces with BIBA, the British and Irish Boxing Authority – the board Lee works for and of which I am a licensed member. In addition, he was attracting some top, top sponsors and going to fund boxing shows in Britain, including one featuring double-Commonwealth title holder Lee McAllister in Scotland. Then came what I thought was a life-changing phone call. He introduced himself as Charles Russo and was happy-go-lucky and upbeat in tone. He apologised for being so hard to get hold of and I was encouraged when he knew about my Guinness World Records.

I asked if he had time to talk and he said he was happy to make time. I told him about my boxing career and my desire to continue fighting. Russo listened and said he would certainly be including me in Boxing at Sea. The prospect of me setting a further world record for being the oldest active professional boxer was a big pull for the show. The conversation ended with him agreeing we needed to have another serious chat.

I was on cloud nine when I rang Lee to say Russo was putting me on the show. And things continued to go well as Russo was back on the line a week later and again speaking very positively. He had lined up a possible opponent – Jimmy 'The Hawk' Lloyd, of Kurdish descent and based in Chester. I had heard the name and asked his age. When Russo said he was 49, that was no problem. Now I know even that information isn't true. But thinking I was giving away 15 years was no big deal compared with some of the much younger opponents I have faced in the last few years.

Russo appeared very considerate as he asked again if the age difference was an issue and I was happy with his proposition. He also promised the money would be very good. The impression he gave was of a man who did things right and was sensitive to the needs of boxers. How wrong could I be?

Two months later Russo made a third call and impressed me still further. He said my fight was not going to be over 12 rounds, as originally thought, but four. This was for insurance reasons and because the safety of older boxers was top priority. This sounded proper. At last, I'd found someone who valued the most important people in boxing.

And that wasn't all. My fight with Jimmy was to be for the inaugural Gold Division world heavyweight title! So here it was, at long last – my chance to end my career as a world champion. Russo said that he originally planned two nights of world championship boxing but had now added a legends night – just for me.

Top names, including Ruddick Bowe and Eric 'Butterbean' Esch, were taking part in bouts of virtual boxing. They would be one side of a giant screen and matched against a member of the audience on the other. This made me worry that he intended my fight to be virtual, and I told him straight that I preferred fights where I can give out and receive pain. "Don't worry, Steve," he said. "Your fight is for real. The screen will be lifted for the main event of the evening – Steve Ward versus Jimmy 'Hawk' Lloyd."

I felt like telling the world but kept the news to a select few. Lucy knew the story from day one; now I shared it with people at the Starbox boxing club where I like to train, close friends and a few members of the media who have followed my career. Everyone was almost as excited as I was, if that's possible. I had continued to keep myself very fit but naturally needed to step up. My usual programme including running, cycling and gym work was fine until Christmas, then on Boxing Day I would become extra serious. May 13, 2021 would be here before I knew it and I needed to be in tip-top condition.

Russo told me my fight would be in the first couple of days of the cruise, so I could then rest my body and enjoy the holiday of a lifetime. In addition, there was talk of the boxers arriving in Miami the month before to test our sea legs. This guy seemed to have thought of everything, and Lucy was thrilled at the whole idea. She envisaged sharing my big moment by walking me to the ring, as she has over recent years, and then enjoying the perfect break from all the hard work she puts in at King's Mill Hospital, particularly during the very difficult times of the Covid-19 pandemic.

The coronavirus, and the lockdowns it brought, was in my thinking, of course. Was May 13 too early for the show to go ahead? I asked the question several times and each time Russo seemed confident of his ground. We spoke, too, about the Guinness Book of World Records. Lucy and I had done the spadework for my previous records, but Russo insisted that he would sort it out. He would talk with the American branch and ensure their support by offering

them a spot on the cruise. He was willing to fund that, because of the prestige of being able to announce a new world
record.

Gradually, though, the red flags started to emerge. Big
and significant enough ones for me to think about, but
not to make me seriously doubt. Lee phoned to say he had
pulled out. There had been a disagreement between BIBA
and the BMMAFU, leading them to go their separate ways.
As someone who worked for BIBA, Lee had been put on
the spot. He had to nail his colours to one mast or the other.
In all honesty, he had little choice but to stick with BIBA.
Fair enough; I understood.

But it wasn't my argument and I wasn't being asked to
choose. I decided to take Russo as I found him and so far,
it was so good. It was only later I discovered the reason for
the split. Russo's promise to fund the McAllister show had
fallen flat. That had left the show's other backers to foot
the bill.

Name-calling followed the split. Nasty things were written on both sides. Knowing how corrupt the sport can be
at a high level, they didn't shock me as much as you would
think. I kept my head down and ploughed on. I contacted
Jimmy and we spoke briefly about publicity. He was happy
to travel to the Midlands and we would stage a pre-fight
event to spread the news. But understandably we held back
on arranging a date until we knew for sure that May 13 had
the green light.

I did my research on "The Hawk" – a six-belt champion.
I had every reason to respect him, as I do anyone prepared
to put their body on the line in the ring. I watched as much
footage of him as I could and worked out my tactics. I was
going to come at him hard from the opening bell, not give

him any time to settle. I spotted his potential weakness and knew I could exploit it. There was no doubt in my mind I was going to beat him. I wasn't going to Boxing at Sea for the money, the world record or the prestige of getting myself better known.

My mission was to be a world champion.

My friend at *Central TV*, Steve Clamp, did me proud. He organised a news report that went out in the Midlands. They lapped up the story of a 64-year-old still boxing and set to create another world record, and they even tracked down Russo to give an interview himself. The item was later repeated on a Sunday-morning show that goes out across the whole *ITV* network.

Me and my fight also got a splash in the *Daily Star* and in local media, who have been so supportive of me throughout. My plan though was to leave most of it until just before May 13. No point in telling the nation, I figured, when there was still time to forget.

Meanwhile the communication with Russo continued, with some of it raising minor alarms. Although money wasn't the issue, of course I wanted to know exactly where I stood. Moving on from initial vague promises it would be "very good", I needed to see it in black and white. I spoke with Russo several times and, on each occasion, the contract was going to be sent to me in a week or so. This was beginning to sound like "the cheque is in the post".

Once he was more forthcoming. He explained that additional sponsorship had come in for the show and he had delayed sending out the contracts because this affected how much the individual boxers were going to be paid. He didn't want us to miss out in any way.

I continued to ask about Covid-19 and the Guinness Book of World Records, and he told me he was scheduling a meeting with the entertainments board about entertainment during the cruise. But he never came back with any conclusions. We were though promised that the well-known American band Atlantic Starr, no less, would be singing the national anthems. That was quite a thought.

Russo said he was meeting with representatives of the cruise liners and I noted from the beginning that he had mentioned one cruise company in particular, Carnival. This time he did return with a result. The show was still on – for now! They would keep a close eye on international developments but expected May 13 would be fine. He did however have later dates as backup. One way or another, he said, Boxing at Sea would happen.

Russo spoke about other shows he was working on, including a street fair in America and one at a hotel in Tulsa on April 24 involving several champions. He was giving the impression he had a lot of events on. As for the Guinness Book of World Records, everything was agreed. But then he came back to me and said he was £700 short and asked if I could find a sponsor. I did.

A friend and businessman not only stomped up the cash, but was willing to sponsor me as well. In addition, 10 friends booked places on the cruise. Nine of them booked rooms and paid a deposit, the other booked a suite and paid in full up front.

With the help of a friend who gave me personal access to a gym to train during lockdown, my preparations were going very well. I was on a very disciplined diet, putting in hours and hours of hard physical work and enjoying almost every minute of it.

A few people probably thought I was mad, seeing me overtake them on my bike and running up hills backwards, but that's me. That's Steve Ward.

The Covid issue however wasn't going away and started to cause more headaches. Okay, the show might be on, but how were we going to get there? And what would we have to do to comply with all the restrictions and regulations? The vaccine was straightforward enough. All boxers needed to have their two jabs in time for the show. I was in a good position to meet that requirement. Due to my age, I was offered the first one in February. I knew all about it afterwards, feeling ill for a few days.

I wouldn't have been due for my second dose until well after May 13, so that was no good. But staff at the vaccination centre were more than happy to help. When I told them about the fight, they pencilled me in, without hesitation, for April 30.

Quarantine was another question. I was concerned about if, and for how long, we would have to go into isolation before and after flying from England. Russo answered that one very simply – each boxer needed to comply with their respective government's orders. With guidance and restrictions changing almost daily, there was no point in me sorting that out too soon. But what of Lucy? That was another matter.

She has an important job which she takes very seriously. She needed to know what holiday she needed to take if she was to make the cruise. With unknowns both before and afterwards, that was no easy matter. The NHS continued, of course, to be extremely busy, so she started to get more concerned. It was beginning to look like I'd be flying out on my own.

That's if there were any flights in the first place. The planned easing of restrictions didn't apply to international travel – or certainly not in time for my fight. I spoke the issue through with Russo. He was promising to fund our travel, but no dates were mentioned. Meanwhile, it was up to us to sort things out.

Elite sportsmen and women were exempt from the travel ban. That's why football teams were still travelling throughout Europe, and England were playing cricket in India. Did I qualify as an elite performer? I queried it with the office of my local MP, Ben Bradley, and they promised to look into it. The answer they brought back was positive. There was no obstacle to me getting on the plane.

The clock was ticking. By now it was clear we weren't going to test our sea legs. It was impractical for several reasons. But everything was still on – at least in my mind – until the last week in March. It was then I received three separate texts and phone calls, each warning me in the strongest possible terms things weren't right. All three held solid positions in the boxing world and, as far as I know, don't know each other.

"Steve, get out, this is a bag of shite," one read. "You are being done left right and centre."

"Steve, fuck it off now," read another. "He's a conman. I have done some research and he is a downright conman."

"He is just there to rip people off," was the third. "You are going to be one of many. He did a rock concert that never took place."

It was a rude shock. The worst of all was a phone call urging me to look at the next issue of *Boxing News*. There the real Charles Russo was exposed. Big time. The article was written by Oliver Fennell, a guy I know and have contact with. To make his article even more powerful, he was in the same boat. He, too, had been taken in hook, line and sinker by Russo.

He gave front page publicity to Russo in the same publication in December 2020 when he thought he had a great scoop. Now he was eating humble pie by admitting his honest mistake.

The story was written under the headline of "Get this man out of boxing now" and Oliver had obviously done his research. He had been given a host of contacts with people who had experience of Russo and his ways. Here is a small extract from Oliver's article that gives you a fair idea…

"Each name I speak to offers more names. If there were one or two, I'd ignore it. Even 10 or 20 I might put down to rivalries or misunderstandings. But there are dozens upon dozens of them, to tell all their stories would require a book. Some are famous, others unknown and they are dotted around the world, but they all have one thing in common – they all talk about Charles Russo and none of them in a good way. I've never met such a tide of ill will against one person."

In short, Russo had allegedly been given a two-year suspended sentence at a fraud and larceny trial at New York's Stapleton Criminal Court in 2015. Fennell argues that Russo was originally known as Peter McMahon, who presented himself as the organiser of a rock concert that never happened. According to the article, a total of 36 bands paid deposits to appear at the show only for McMahon, or Russo, to disappear a few days before the due date with their money.

The trail then went on to modelling where Hannah

Sargeant, a model from Kentucky, posted a warning on Facebook in March 2017 claiming Charles Russo, of Charlie's Angels modelling agency, was Peter McMahon and accusing him of "conning people for years." From there, he went into boxing and has been accused of trying to exploit Lisa McClellan, the sister of Gerald, the boxer so badly injured in that infamous fight with Nigel Benn in 1995.

Lisa says that Russo approached her with offers of help from his boxing union when she and Gerald, whom she cares for, were staying in a hotel whilst their bathroom was being modified so he could use it more easily. Russo not only didn't pay, she claims, but later caused her still more grief after she told him she didn't believe that either his boxing union or his attorney existed.

There was enough in that article – which you can read in full online – to open my eyes and 99 per cent convince me that I'd been conned. But I still needed to do my own research and check it out for myself. I then found out that the cruise line companies in the Bahamas were not allowed to sail until June 1 at the earliest.

As soon as I saw the report, I began my own research. Having picked up the name of the cruise liner company mentioned in my talks with Russo, I phoned them to ask if they knew anything about either him or Boxing at Sea. They told me they had never heard of him and there was no question of there being any booking.

I asked also if it was possible the event had been booked with any other cruise liner company and was told that was impossible. It was the same story with the Guinness Book of Records. I phoned the English branch and they promised to liaise with their American colleagues. You can probably guess the answer that came back. Again, no contact had ever been made by Russo and they knew nothing about him or Boxing at Sea.

People like Russo probably haven't any idea of how many people they let down and how many lives they are messing with when they devise things like this. In my case, I had 10 people due to fly out from England to support me and be part of the cruise. All of these were very much looking forward to what seemed like a trip of a lifetime.

In the weeks after the personal revelations and the *Boxing News* article, I must admit I started to have silly thoughts. I'd been promised what seemed like the world and now, in a flicking of an eyelid, it had all been taken away from me. At 64 years old, Russo had robbed me of my last chance.

But I had responsibilities – not least to those who had booked on the so-called cruise to support me. Telling them what had happened was very painful; each time I went through the story, it was like twisting a knife in my personal wounds. But I had to do it because everyone deserved a proper explanation, even if they might go away thinking less of me for being taken for a fool.

I made eight personal visits and made lengthy phone calls to the other two. I told them the honest truth, that I was one of many people taken for a fool by Russo, and apologised for the fact that they had now become involved. They were good with me and understood. All of them accepted I had been acting in good faith and in three or four cases, I paid the deposits back myself because I knew they were people who didn't have money to waste.

Friends asked me: "Is there any way you are mistaken, Steve, and Russo is legit?" I told them that unfortunately

I now knew the truth beyond any reasonable doubt. I was contacted by several people from the media, including contacts I knew, and had to give them the same answer. I was told not to comment because no offence will have taken place until after the date of May 13, when the non-event was due to happen.

I was told that the FBI wished to interview me in London as they were investigating Russo but again, I decided to keep my mouth shut until later. In the weeks that followed, I waited for Russo to contact me. I didn't want him to know I was fully aware by now of what kind of character he was and that I thought his event was a sham. But I was told to record any conversations I had with him and play along with whatever he said.

He made a firm promise to phone me one day in mid-April but then made an excuse that he was very busy and that he would be in touch later. The second call didn't happen either. Eventually it became clear he knew that I knew. The message had probably got back from one of my friends who was determined to act against him. Some of my friends have managed to get their money back via the banks, and Russo had the barefaced cheek to message me to complain about that.

With the benefit of hindsight, I should have used my head instead of my heart. When Russo presented his vision to me, it was so, so prim and proper. It seemed perfect. But that's not the way things are in boxing. My experience tells me that nothing falls so easily into place in this sport. Nothing happens in boxing without a battle.

In all honesty, I don't want to waste one more second on him. If and when I get my chance to speak with the authorities, I will gladly do so. All I can say is that I hope that justice will be done. I'm no longer thinking so much about myself but the many others whose lives he has tampered with. I believe what goes around comes around and for Charles Russo, that's not going to be pleasant.

Boxing at Sea was going to be the last chapter in my book – the one where my long rollercoaster career came to a climax. But Keith Large was right when he said: "The bigger the knockback, the bigger the comeback!"

11

ON TOP OF THE WORLD

By Keith Large, producer of multi-international award-win-
ning documentary **The Champ of Champs**
I'm writing this the morning after I spoke to Steve to discuss the
heartbreaking news. His dream fight, to win a world title on a
cruise ship in the Bahamas has vanished ... along with the promise
of a follow-up fight, on the day before his 65th birthday, against
a multi-weight world champion known as 'Superman'.
I've never met Roy Jones Junior or Christopher Reeve, but in
January 2019 I did meet Superman. There was no telephone box
for him to get changed. This was something far more magical. A
roadside café decorated in boxing memorabilia and dedicated to
the world's oldest active professional boxer.
I knew Mark, the café owner, and he knew I produced films.
We'd just won an award in Hollywood and I was getting a lot of
offers to produce fiction films. Documentaries interested me,
but it was not the right time ... or so I thought! I was on the crest of
the wave with short fiction and it didn't seem the right moment to
change direction.
Mark kept saying: "You need to make a documentary about
Steve." Out of politeness to Mark, I agreed to meet Steve. Sat
across the table in Champs Café, Steve recalled the story of how a
tonne and a quarter of concrete crushed his foot. Seven UK medi-
cal specialists had told him he'd never be able to walk properly

again. He vowed to fight on. He would find a way to walk properly again. With a promise of when he did, he would return to the ring. In Hollywood, Superman is a work of fiction. In the East Midlands, he is real.

Within hours of meeting Steve, I'd put together a crew to make The Champ of Champs. Over the next couple of years, I had many meetings with Steve and spent endless hours talking to him. He is a man of so many qualities, including the ones I value most – reliable, honest and trustworthy. Yet it is the characteristic of resilience that ultimately defines this Superman.

When we ended our telephone conversation about the cancelled cruise fight, Steve already had another world title fight lined up. This is the Steve Ward I have got to know. The bigger the knockback, the bigger the comeback.

***

By Lee Murtagh, former Irish super welterweight champion and BIBA head of ring officials
I first came across Steve Ward when refereeing at an English Boxing Federation show in Derby. I didn't know much about him, to be honest, but he cracked me up when he came up to me to say thank you after winning his fight.

When he told me "54", I thought it was his favourite number – I didn't realise it was his age! Afterwards I looked him up and found out he had come back into the ring after a professional career that had started well and had then seen him thrown in with some very good fighters.

I then refereed more of his fights with the EBF as he wrote himself into the Guinness Book of World Records.

Since then, he came back into my life through a series of random phone calls and I was there as a judge when he fought the dangerous Jodie Meikle. The matchmaking wasn't good against a boxer in his thirties and Steve lost.

But even that was far from the end for Steve Ward, The Legend. I was the referee when he fought Andreas Sidon in 2017, and that was a great occasion for Mansfield. Sidon was a serious fighter who had beaten Danny Williams, the guy who knocked out Mike Tyson, and looking back, a lot was in the German's favour. He was a more natural heavyweight than Steve and usually a good big 'un will beat a good little 'un.

But Steve came so close to giving his fans the perfect ending. All three judges had Steve well ahead and I could see Sidon was in a daze after being caught with a right hand on his cheekbone. I didn't catch on at first when Steve suffered his shoulder injury. I thought he was trying a karate move and he was still jabbing away.

But when I realised what had happened, I had no choice but to stop the fight. When my girlfriend and I spoke to Steve about the possibility of a film on his career, we got the idea he wanted to box again. So when I was made head referee for the proposed Boxing at Sea idea, I spoke with Steve and we had a group chat with the promoter, Charles Russo.

Steve was preparing for a fight for a world title, when I told him I had found out Russo wasn't genuine. We now have another film to follow: 'The Straightener' ... 'Scam at Sea'.

Another fight in Cyprus then fell through before the World Legends Championship was formed and Steve was lined up to fight Romanian Adrian Parlogea. There could be no better place for such an occasion than Mansfield in front of Steve's fans.

There were plenty of obstacles to overcome before the big night but the show itself was great. Perhaps even better than the Andreas Sidon fight. Adrian was no mug. He had 300 amateur fights before turning pro in his thirties and had been part of the Romanian national team. He had the potential to make Steve work. But Steve didn't fight like I thought he would...

After beginning to come to terms with the idea the exposure of Boxing at Sea meant the end of the road, I had a further disappointment with Plan B. A promoter from Cyprus had been in touch with Lee Murtagh to offer me a fight against South African Toto Mugambe, close to my 65th birthday.

For a while, this looked likely to happen. An international casino in Nicosia was the venue with a suitable date on the table. But the uncertainties surrounding Covid-19 and restrictions caused another change of plan. When the fight was put back to October 2021, I could have been a clever dick and tried to get round my 65th birthday being the end of my career. But I didn't want to do so.

I have vowed more than once that this was my last fight, but this time I mean it. I wasn't prepared to commit to anything after my birthday, so Cyprus also bit the dust. The next stop was Oxford. A promoter spoke with Lee about staging a world title fight at a venue that clearly wasn't large enough. His next move was to say: "If I can get Steve Ward to fight for a world title, I will get a bigger venue."

I wasn't getting good vibes about this one. To be honest, I never even found out the promoter's name – I didn't want to know anything about him. It appeared he wasn't willing to listen to people with vast experience and I could see this plan coming unstuck. Having already suffered two setbacks, I couldn't take the risk of this one falling flat as well. So, I decided it wasn't for me.

There was talk of a fight in Leeds before Lee stepped up to the plate. Instead of acting as a go-between, he took the issue of organising a fight into his own hands. Why Leeds, we thought, when we remembered that fantastic night in Mansfield in 2017? So, with the considerable help of his mother, a boxing promoter, my final, final fight and my last chance of landing a world title started to take shape.

I wanted the fight to be for a title and Lee said it would be for the World Legends Championship. A nice idea, but he and his mum had to jump through many hoops to make that possible. Firstly, they had to get representatives from other countries in place. They managed it, with people from 12 to 14 countries getting on board. Then BIBA was agreed as the sanctioning body and the Association of Professional Boxing Commissions as the commissioning body.

My fight against 50-year-old Romanian Adrian Parlogea was to be for the inaugural World Gold Division Legends Championship, which in future will include fights at all weights – with a bronze belt for boxers between 30 and 40, silver for 40 to 50-year-olds and gold for 50 to 65-year-olds. This new venture in boxing is exciting in many ways and I now plan to be involved in future years. The established boxing boards didn't help because, in my opinion, they feel threatened by it.

The potential for legends boxing was highlighted in November 2020 when two great world heavyweight champions, Mike Tyson and Roy Jones Junior, took part in an exhibition fight in Los Angeles. Neither fighter was able to get a licence to fight professionally, so it took place as an exhibition. Yet the huge numbers of people viewing and taking an interest in the fight across the world tells its own story. And I know there are many other boxers itching to get back into the ring who will be delighted they can now do so.

Health naturally comes first. Veteran boxers can only take part by passing the same very stringent medical as other fighters, and only boxers in A1 condition will be involved. So amazingly, after seeing what would have been completely new ground for boxing crash when Boxing at Sea was exposed, I found myself at the centre of another piece of boxing history a few weeks later.

I was left with around six weeks to prepare for the big fight, which was fine as I had been in full fight-mode training anyway since Boxing Day. But the toll it was taking on me was increasing all the time. That made me decide there was no way I could any longer put my body through such a gruelling test and it wasn't fair on my wife, either. Me coming home after a hard day's training has never been a pretty sight, but she has witnessed how hard this was for me.

In the first three weeks of training, I lost two and a half stones to comfortably come down to under the fight limit of 14 stones four pounds. This is a flavour of my daily schedule...

4am: Get up, have a small glass of water and be out of the house by 4.15am. First task was a run. I estimated it to be between 12 and 14 miles. The run included hills, and half of it was done backwards. My training kit ensured I sweated as much as possible and included a wetsuit, tracksuit bottoms, bin-liner, furry top and, most importantly, a woolly hat.

Back home at around 6am, I then did about 20 minutes on the skipping rope, followed by an hour of body exercises. These included squats, sit-ups and leg raises, plus a couple of exercises I particularly designed for myself.

Afterwards I went into the lounge, got stripped off, put my clothes in the washer, had an ice-cold shower and put my work clothes on. Breakfast was bran flakes and raisins – I hated it, but I was eating so little I needed something to keep my bowels moving.

I set off around 7.20am to drive to work. I did a very physical four-hour shift, packing, unloading and offloading. I normally got there early and started immediately. I was literally on the go all the time – packing, moving around and stretching. I didn't take any breaks or socialise. There were only two others in the building – the gaffer in the office and another doing the same job as me. He was usually at one end of the warehouse whilst I was at the other. Usually I didn't have any refreshments, although occasionally I took an energy drink.

I left work at 12.30pm, got back home about 1.10pm and was out of the house again 10 minutes later. Time for another run, aimed at keeping me agile rather than being fast. I mixed up this run, which was about five or six miles, with hopscotch and other exercises to maintain mobility. By this time, I was feeling the effects of my morning routine.

Returning home about 2.30pm, I then repeated the skipping rope and body exercises. The latter involved me hurting myself and sometimes I had blood in my urine. These are minor blood vessels that burst but healed within hours. I had a rest about 4pm. It was also time for my main meal of the day – usually two chicken fillets and vegetables. I had a full pint of water, usually just my second drink of the day, and sometimes laid on the bed for a snooze.

I was up about 5pm when Lucy returned from work. Then we got the chance to talk about the events of the day. At 5.50pm, I put my training kit back on and went to Starbox, the nearest boxing gym. I started with 30 minutes on the bike, pushing it pretty hard. I was absolutely dripping with sweat. Then it was the rowing machine and weights. I didn't do massive weights but high repetitions, because there was no need to bulk me up. Then it was the leg press machine before my favourite; the wallbag.

I treated that like the fight. I used a timer to measure eight three-minute 'rounds', with a minute in between. That was the schedule of the fight. Despite the weight loss, I was finding myself hitting very hard – harder than at any time in my career. I then sparred with a couple of professionals, one of whom was roughly the same size as my opponent. Whilst at the gym, I had a pint of water.

My gym sessions were scheduled to end at 8pm, but sometimes it was more like 8.30pm. The gym is very close to home, but I returned via a five-mile run. I did this run as quickly as I can, but I was so shattered. Near home, there was one house where I ran up and down the steps. Nobody noticed.

I was back home around 9.10pm. Time for a drink. My mouth got very dry during the day, so I had a freezer full of ice pops. I usually had six or seven to make my mouth tingle. The evening was when I felt what I had done most. I relaxed with Lucy catching up on the soaps, *Coronation Street* and *Emmerdale*. Sometimes I fell asleep.

I went to bed about midnight and had difficulty in going to sleep straightaway.

***

I approached the Parlogea fight completely differently to others in recent years. This was no ordinary fight – this was my last fight, with a world title on the line and no room for cock-ups. Either I was going to win and achieve my lifetime ambition of becoming a world champion, or I would walk away defeated. Whatever the result, there would be no second chances.

I didn't want to know anything about the Romanian. Nothing at all. Usually, I'd do my research and work out a battle plan – look for his weakness and know exactly what I need to do from the bell went. Not this time. All I knew before going into the ring was that he was 50 years old, a Romanian and had last been active in the ring in 2019.

Parlogea arrived in England 10 days before the fight. He then needed to quarantine and take about three Covid tests before the fight on August 6. I had tests to do myself but couldn't afford to waste time and energy worrying about the possibility it could all be called off. After all that had gone before, I decided that this was it. This was going to happen.

My plan was to allow my opponent to dictate a little, so I could see what he had got. Did he move well? What was his best punch? What did he like to throw? I would know the answers to all these questions and more come the bell. Then I would come at him very heavily from round two.

The one thing I told Lee Murtagh when the fight was agreed was that I didn't want a repeat of the Andreas Sidon show. Partly because I was also the organiser, I'd found myself literally selling tickets on fight day. This time I wanted to be left alone to concentrate fully on the task in hand. But there were still plenty of obstacles for me to overcome before the fight night at Mansfield Rugby Club.

With time fast running out, tickets weren't selling well – partly a sign of the strange times we had been living in. They were only available online, and I knew this wasn't everyone's cup of tea. Some expressed safety concerns such as would there be Covid-19 track and trace at the venue? This could well be the first time some had been in a big crowd for many months, and it was understandable that some felt a little apprehensive.

Also, with the restrictions only recently having been lifted, people were booking foreign holidays. With their hard-earned break on the line if they tested positive, were they willing to risk a night out? The 450 capacity was out of the window, the aim now was to break even.

In the last few days, I did my bit – making phone calls, speaking with people, trying to spread the word that Stevie Ward was fighting for a world title in Mansfield. It went well and I even ended up delivering tickets until about midnight with less than a week to go.

At the same time, I was fighting another battle; one I had not made public. Doctors told me a few years ago that my body was riddled with arthritis, particularly the neck. A symptom of the fact that age was getting to me. But I did everything I could to stop it affecting me. When I finished training, I had my shower, put on the creams and gave myself infrared treatment. In the past, that would have eased the pain. But it was still with me next morning when I loosened up to reduce its impact.

In the last days before the big fight, I was neither excited nor nervous. Instead, I couldn't wait for the big night. I wanted it to be there and then. But with about five days left, I almost passed out in the gym. I had driven myself to my cut off point and beyond so many times. I sat myself down; not only to compose myself physically, but also to have a good think.

I asked myself one more time if this was all worth it? How far was I prepared to go to achieve my aim? Could I punch hard for the full 24 minutes, if I needed to? Hard enough to knock this man out?

I knew the answer to the last two questions was "yes."

Then, just five days before the big night, came potentially devastating news. For the second time, Lucy told me out of the blue that my world record for the oldest professional boxer had been officially beaten.

I knew a 70-year-old called Albert Hughes had made claim to my record after a fight in Indianapolis in December 2019. The circumstances were strange as Hughes returned to the ring after 36 years and knocked out a 43-year-old. He did it to fulfil the dying wish of his son, to create a world record, but there was a question mark over if it was a proper fight.

I was shocked Guinness had now accepted this as a record and the timing, so close to my fight, was unbelievable. Lucy was more upset than I was. I managed to put it into perspective; I was aiming to win a world title and knowing I was still the oldest active boxer. Sadly, both Hughes and his son have since passed away and that is one reason I will not be contesting it. If I complained, it would look as if I was the bad guy. That's not me. In the circumstances, we should let it go.

At the time, and with such an important battle to win, I simply couldn't afford to give the disappointment too much thought. I finished my training on the Tuesday evening before the Friday night fight, knowing a few days of rest was important as part of my preparation. The weigh-in the day before was very different. Because of my opponent's isolation, he had to be weighed where he was staying whilst I went to Starbox to go on the scales at the same time. That was fine with me; I had no desire to set eyes on Parlogea. I weighed 13 stone seven pounds, my opponent 13 stone two and a quarter.

I had a sports massage with my cornerman and physiotherapist, Paul, who confirmed that my shoulder was holding up well, and then watched TV in the evening. Sleeping that night wasn't easy with such a huge day on my mind. I got up and made sure my clothing and other bits were ready before having a ride out. Lucy knew I would be in no mood for talking to anyone, so it was better I was on my own.

I'd thought about going to Critchley, a lovely village near the Crich tram museum and having a light breakfast at the bakery. Unfortunately, the café was shut. A bad omen? I couldn't afford to chase that thought. Instead I drove on to Matlock Bath, where I had something to eat beside the river. That passed some peaceful time before driving home in the early afternoon.

Lucy was out with her mother so after putting my stuff in the car, I went to bed. I relaxed but was too alert to sleep. Lucy came home and we had a cup of tea and a chit chat about the fight. I didn't want anything more to eat. No need to get to the venue too early because there can be a lot of waiting around, and I preferred not to talk to people if I could avoid it.

The show included a six-fight undercard due to start at eight o'clock and when we arrived at about 7.10pm, the car park was already packed almost solid. Luckily, we found room to park near the entrance. There were plenty of people around when I walked into the hall and I made my way to the changing room where Lucy joined me.

The main fight was scheduled for 10 o'clock, with a medical fixed for 8.30pm. That was the first time I had set eyes on the Romanian and it wasn't the friendliest of occasions. In fact, there was very nearly not an official fight at all. It looked like we were going to settle it there and then.

Getting involved with my opponent is not my style but Parlogea did everything possible to provoke me. When I passed near him, he grunted and groaned. He was speaking in his own language but I was getting the message, and it wasn't nice. This guy was doing himself no favours.

Then he tried to shoulder me as we passed and I retaliated by pushing him. That sent him flying across the room. For a few seconds, I thought there was going to be no need to get into the ring.

That incident totally changed my tactics for the evening. Back in the changing room, I told my coach Paul there was no way I was going to take my time. I would come for him from the first bell. He had seriously annoyed me and had it coming.

I wasn't so much counting the minutes down to the fight as the seconds, and I asked my team several times to go into the hall and check on the progress of the fights. When I knew they were into the sixth and final bout, I got myself warmed up to the point where I was sweating. That way I would be 100 per cent ready as soon as I climbed into the ring. Paul told me the Romanian was going to wonder what had hit him. He knew I would set a fast pace. Then came the words I was waiting for: "Okay, Steve ... we are ready for you!"

That was the signal for Lucy, the lead girl, and Tammy to go into the main hall with the Union Jack, followed by me with my hood up, and Kim and Lizzy holding the Mansfield and Nottingham flags. Again, I had *Heart's on Fire* as my welcome music. I like to listen to the beginning before making my way to the ring. Only when it got to a particular point did I start my walk.

I could immediately tell that the atmosphere was great.

Cheers went up to greet me. Everything was going to plan with me being second into the ring. But Parlogea did pull one trick, presumably to annoy me. I was due in the blue corner but, when I climbed into the ring, he was there. I wasn't going to allow that to wind me up. I was focused and ready to get on with it.

I held my hands to touch gloves with him but again I detected a lack of respect when the national anthems were played. He had been jigging about on the spot in his corner before standing still to mark the Romanian anthem. But when *God Save The Queen* was played, he was moving about again. I didn't like that.

Referee Lee Murtagh pulled us into the centre of the ring to give us our instructions. Parlogea tried to knock me as we touched gloves but I wasn't playing. I knew something he didn't – I was going to smash the hell out of him.

I heard the master of ceremonies announce the final words: "Let's get ready to make history." That had a double meaning for me. I was aiming to create history by becoming the oldest ever world champion and this was, of course, the first ever World Legends Championship fight.

As soon as the bell went, I flew over and got into his face straightaway. I didn't want to give him any time to get settled or find his rhythm. I knew this guy could be awkward if the fight went the distance.

I'm not sure Parlogea knew what to expect. It certainly wasn't a man of nearly 65 who came out of that corner. I may not have been as quick on my feet as I once was, but I was super fit and packing the heaviest punch of my life. I threw punches from all angles and within 30 seconds he hit the floor after a series of combinations. Parlogea took the full eight count before the referee asked him if he was okay to carry on. "Yes!" he snapped, curtly. I knew I had hurt him and wanted to follow it up as quickly as possible.

Again, I was hitting him from all angles. In return, he landed a couple of decent punches but in the frame of mind I was in, neither really registered, let alone hurt me. I was totally in the zone, focused on putting him away.

The Romanian tried dirty tactics by tying me up and hitting me on the side of the head. So, I responded by doing the same to him. The referee intervened and told us to keep it clean. But soon enough, I caught him again with both a right and a left. Parlogea went down for a second time. For a couple of seconds, I stood over him rather than going back to the neutral corner, which gave him slightly more time to recover. Again, he answered yes when the referee asked if he wanted to continue after the full count.

There was an exchange of blows and he was near the ropes. I connected with a fierce right and shaped to follow up with a left. But as he leant over the ropes, I connected instead with my forearm to his chest, causing him to over-balance. He fell out of the ring and onto the judges' table, with his legs in the air. I quickly put my hand on his knee to steady him in case he slipped backwards. I didn't want to win that way. The referee rightly didn't score it as a knock-down, but I knew the Romanian was in big trouble. And there was no escape.

For a third time, he answered snappily that he was happy to box on. But his dazed eyes were telling me a different story. I couldn't afford to show any mercy. This was my chance to finish him. So, I went straight back over to him and hit him with a series of punches. I knew I was hurting him.

A left landed on his chin, followed by a right – and he was down for a third time. The referee counted nine, then asked if he was alright. This time there was no answer. He asked again and still there was no reply just a glazed look. At that moment, I knew I had done it. I had won with a knockout after two minutes and 59 seconds of round one.

I dropped onto my knees in the neutral corner and the enormity of what had just happened began to hit me. "Oh my God, oh my God," I thought to myself. "I've done it!" The feeling was unreal. I may have been confident, but it was still a shock in a way. It brought a lump to my throat.

The master of ceremonies announced the official result and when I went over to Parlogea, all the nastiness was gone. "Well done, mate," I said. "Good lad, top fighter." I don't think he knew where he was – his eyes still looked very distant. The referee called us both into the centre of the ring and announced the words that were music to my ears. "The winner and the new cruiserweight World Legends champion – Stevie 'the Legend' Ward!"

Wow! What a moment. It's a big old world, with billions of people, and I was world champion. Lucy climbed into the ring to give me a kiss and congratulate me. I couldn't have done this without her.

I thought about Dad. He should have been there to see me do what he had predicted all those years ago. "You will be seeing me on Wednesday, Dad," I said in my mind. I was going to visit him at Bulwell Cemetery.

I was feeling jubilant; as happy as Larry! Photos were taken and interviews done in the ring. I didn't know which organisations they were representing. That didn't matter. As I had planned, I had a pint of lager shandy in the ring. Or a part of three different pints. Some might think that's not what a boxer should do. But I was now a former boxer – and I think I had earnt it.

***

*By Mike Weaver, former WBA world heavyweight champion
and chairman of the World Legends Championship*
*Congratulations to Steve 'The Legend' Ward on becoming the
first ever World Legends champion. Boxers share a mutual respect when they put their bodies on the line inside the ring and
when I heard about Steve as the world's oldest active professional
boxer, and still fighting a few days before his 65th birthday, I
was amazed.*
*This record-breaking man has proven to the world that age can
really be just a number. Hopefully, the World Legends Championship will welcome back many great boxers in future – but
whatever happens, Steve Ward will go down in history as our
pioneer.*

A strange thing happened when I finally climbed out of the
ring. Taking my first step, I was still feeling jubilant. But
that feeling was replaced with a sense of great sadness as I
took my second. Suddenly it struck me that I was doing this
for the last time. Never again would I step into a boxing
ring after all these years. The thought genuinely brought a
tear to my eyes.

I have lived and bled for boxing. Everything about me
has been centred on boxing. Now, at a stroke, that was all
in the past. Happily, the jubilant feeling then overcame the
sadness again and I enjoyed the rest of the evening. I spoke
with as many people in the hall as I could. I'm sorry if I was
unable to get round to you, if you were there.

There was also some filming to do and more interviews.
It was around 1.45am before we left the building and in
the next day or so, I enjoyed the biggest portion of fish and
chips I can remember. There was a fish and chip shop di-

rectly opposite Starbox gym, and it was another treat I had promised myself during those gruelling days of training.

But there's no way I'm going to let myself go, and I was back in the gym on the Sunday. Not training like I would for a fight but keeping myself fit. I feel better and healthier for losing the three stones and intend to keep the weight off.

The interviews kept coming and I had about 20 media contacts by the following Tuesday. Again, I didn't always know who they were working for. I'd agreed in advance of the fight not to speak with any other national newspapers after being contacted a few weeks previously and interviewed by *The Sun*. But one journalist forwarded his article onto the *Daily Mirror* and a very good article, with a great photograph of me and my team, took up almost the whole of page 25 on the Tuesday.

A PR agency got in touch, offering to help me deal with the media at no expense. I said a thankful yes. It was through them that an interview was arranged with *ITV*. And there I was on the Thursday as the last items on the famous *BBC News at Ten*. I was back on the BBC on the Saturday morning, on Claudia Winkelman's show on *Radio 2*. The presenter, Rob Beckett, compared me with Benjamin Button!

I was happy to talk about what I had done but, as for my plans for the future, I wanted to be left alone. I told everyone to give me a few weeks to think things over. Yes, I have some idea – some plans I hope will come to fruition – but I didn't want to commit myself.

Countless people phoned or messaged to congratulate me. I thank you all. It was also wonderful walking down the local high street and seeing "Steve Ward, we love you" in one of the shop windows. On several occasions, I was told in shops to keep my money in my pocket.

The people of Nottingham and Mansfield will always mean everything to me. I'm so glad now that my boxing career ended in my hometown. I've finished as a world champion and triple Guinness Book of World Records holder. I have my legacy.

In the end, my boxing career spanned 56 years and I can honestly say I've loved all of it. It was a reluctant Steve Ward my dad first took to the Nottingham School of Boxing, but I'd happily do the same thing all over again. For now, though, I'll settle for being the only world champion with a bus pass!

WHAT NEXT FOR THE LEGEND?

By Mick Barton, head of the independent group on Mansfield District Council.

I've known Steve Ward since he was working on the doors of local pubs and clubs. We became mates and when he continued his boxing career, I always supported him, buying tickets and sponsoring his fights – including when he fought for a world title in Mansfield in 2017.

The people of Mansfield are very proud of Steve and all his achievements, but I also know Steve's qualities as a person. He is genuine, will do anything for anybody and has a heart of gold. That's why I would like him to be a councillor.

Steve is someone who wants to help people and offers a lot to the community. He took up my offer of standing as a councillor in the 2019 election and he did very well. He lost a seat in the Ransom Wood ward, where there is a long-standing Labour councillor, by the small matter of 14 votes.

Steve Ward is a community-spirited man, and I'm sure he will continue to be so.

I can forgive people for taking my retirement from fighting with a pinch of salt. After all, I've had more comebacks than Frank Sinatra. But I do know one thing – I haven't retired from life. There's a great future ahead for me after boxing, and Lucy and I will continue to be a very proud part of the Mansfield community.

I couldn't believe how people turned out to support me when the film *Champ of Champs* was released. We had a big launch night at the John Fretwell Centre, with my friend Tony Delahunty as the master of ceremonies. The event was a tribute to the work put into the film by producer and director Keith Large and it's been amazing to see it win so many film awards.

Whilst we have been writing this book, I have mentioned to him the possibility of a *Champ of Champs II* because my story has moved on in 2021. So, one way or another, with the film and now this book, I hope to get the chance to tell my story to more and more people.

What else I will do is still up in the air. Whether I will have another go at getting on the council, we'll have to wait and see. That was something that had never occurred to me before Mick Barton suggested it. I've got no interest in politics whatsoever, so what use would I be? He thought differently and I had a very interesting experience contesting a seat at the 2019 election.

Mick gave me one of the roughest estates in Mansfield in Ransom Wood. When I say 'rough' I'm not being disrespectful to the people. I'm one of the first to admit that Hyson Green, where I was brought up, was like that too, but I love the people. The area I'm talking about has a derelict look to it in terms of housing and the shops – there was just one whilst I was canvassing there, and that closed early. All that means to me is that the people can do with any help they can get.

I gave my word to Mick that I would leaflet the estate properly and most of it was great. I either put leaflets

THE LEGEND: STEVE WARD

through the doors when there was no answer or had a chat with residents when there was. I think they were surprised by what I told them. I could tell they weren't overly impressed by politics, but neither am I. All I said was that if they had any sensible requests for help, I would do my very best for them. If they made any silly requests, I'd tell them where to go. "That's good enough for me, you've got my vote!" was a typical response.

One or two, however, weren't so easily convinced. I was on the estate one day when a bloke, probably in his thirties and about my size, came marching over towards me. "Did you f****** do this?" he asked. At first, I thought he was talking to someone else, but soon realised he meant the leaflet through his door. And that his target was me.

When I told him all I was doing was leafleting for the election, he got more and more angry. "I'm going to f****** kill you!" he said. Unfortunately for him, he had picked on the wrong man.

I had no reason to want to fight with him and put a bit of distance between us. But he then pulled out a machete and started waving it at me like Zorro. Now I had to defend myself. He made a big mistake by presenting an open target and, using my martial arts skills, I kicked him and then punched him onto the ground, where he lay moaning and groaning. I don't suppose he voted for me, but he probably got the message.

As far as I was concerned, the issue was over and done with and I didn't report it to the police. Mick was surprised and said I should have done so, and then I got a call from security on the estate. They were worried about my safety and suggested I shouldn't go back to the estate anymore. I said I had given my word that I would leaflet the whole of the estate properly and I was going back the next day. It didn't bother me at all whether I bumped into Zorro again.

They were also concerned about how badly I'd hurt him, and I explained that I'd stopped him in his tracks but hadn't maimed him. I had a similar conversation with the police and they were more worried about me. This was a one-off. It wasn't going to stop me doing my job and I continued to talk with people.

When the election took place, it was very close. I was told I had lost by 17 votes and I was asked whether I'd like a recount. That ended up with the Labour councillor beating me by just 14. Maybe if I'd had another five recounts, I would have won! The Labour councillor was very relieved and remarked on how well I had done. I know that Mick would like me to have another go, but I'm not committing myself at this stage.

What I do know is that the people of Mansfield deserve support from their councillors. When I saw women struggling with shopping trolleys, I went to help them. I didn't want a prize; that's the way I was brought up. Similarly, when they took a while to answer the door, I asked whether they were okay or needed any help.

All I can guarantee in my future is that I will learn from experience. I know it's possible to fall into a deep depression after retiring from sport. Some boxers have hit the bottle to attempt to numb the effects. That's not my way. I've been through depression bad enough to consider taking my own life. I know what that feels like, and how it's possible to go down and down.

But that's not going to be me.

ACKNOWLEDGEMENTS

When my dad introduced a scrawny, bullied nine-year-old to Nottingham School of Boxing, he told anyone who cared to listen that Steve Ward would one day be world champion.

I won 136 out of 148 amateur fights. Then, after the death of my dad and a mixed professional career, I retired at the age of 32, feeling let down by the whole boxing business. My life journey since has been full of incredible highs and desperate lows. I got my name into the Guinness Book of World Records three times, after returning to boxing aged 54, and have pursued my dream of becoming an official world champion.

Today the name Steve Ward, of Mansfield stands proudly above some of the greatest in the history of boxing in the list of the 10 oldest active professional boxers. And this is the right time to put my life into print.

In truth, it's the second time. I worked with Richard Longstaff seven or eight years ago. We got on great, had friendly get-togethers and Richard made his notes. Then tragedy struck. Richard fell ill and, soon afterwards, died. He left behind great work which is now part of this book. It's strange how things work out. Back then, my book would have been incomplete. So much has happened since, and still is!

I contacted Richard's daughter, Holly, to tell her about this book, and she was thrilled. She knows her father would be, too, because all his hard work wasn't in vain. Wherever you are, Richard, I appreciate you and all you have done.

Before the book came the film! I was approached a few years ago by Leicestershire film-maker Keith Large, who was interested in producing a documentary film about my life. Apparently random events led to it happening, as Mark Waddingham wrote earlier in the book. *Champ of Champs* included contributions by several important people in my life, such as media man Tony Delahunty, of Mansfield 103.2FM; Marcellus Baz, representing Nottingham School of Boxing; Jamie Hemmings, of Superstar Speakers; and my wife and biggest fan, Lucy. There was footage from my big fight with German giant Andreas Sidon, a roundup of my boxing career and the story of how the sport has changed my life.

The premiere at John Fretwell Centre in Mansfield in 2019 was a glittering occasion. I was so proud when Lucy and I got a standing ovation. The people of Mansfield have always been brilliant to me. The film is a brilliant piece of work, so well put together and has now won 38 international awards – and counting.

As I was beginning work on this book, I heard the great news that it had scooped the prizes of 'best documentary' and 'best producer' at the world-renowned Cannes Film Festival. I don't think even Keith believes how well it's done and, if it wasn't for Covid-19, we may well have been off to France to celebrate.

It was Keith who put me in touch with his ghostwriter friend John Brindley, who worked with me for months to bring my story up to date – after I became the World Legends champion and fulfilled my dad's prediction, just a few days before my 65th birthday. John and I spent many an enjoyable Tuesday afternoon together and I'd like to thank all of you who have helped us to produce *The Legend.*

It has been a great privilege for me that two very big names in the world of heavyweight boxing have written such kind words about me – so thank you to Danny Williams for the foreword, and to Mike Weaver for his tribute. Thanks also to Jimmy 'the Hawk' Lloyd – I never met you in the ring, but we share a mutual respect – and to my friend and international boxing referee Lee Murtagh, for his written contributions and a part in my two world title fights in Mansfield.

They are among the direct contributors to my story – a list that also includes no fewer than three civic heads and another local politician in Tony Eggington, Michael Wildgust, Kate Allsopp and Mick Barton.

Thank you, too, to my close friend Steve Clamp from *Central TV*, for all the interviews and fight footage; Owen Shipton from *Notts TV*, for covering both title fights; John Lomas, sports writer for the *Mansfield Chad* and *Hucknall Dispatch;* and Martin Fricker, for writing the article that went in the *Daily Mirror.*

Joining Tony Delahunty among the media who have helped me has been Oliver Fennell, of *Boxing News;* a man who was big enough to admit he had also been taken in by Charles Russo and set the record straight. I was delighted that Marcellus Baz wrote his piece to highlight where my boxing story began all those years ago at the Nottingham School of Boxing.

And as I conclude my thanks, I'm coming to some of the most important people of all. My wife Louisa, or Lucy, has backed me with my book, just as she has backed me in every way since we got together. As well as her written contributions, she has done a lot of proofreading and editing to help with the finished article.

Kev Henshaw, of Starbox gym, has also been brilliant. As well as providing me with a place to train, his venue has also been used for interviews and photographs. And, of course, *The Legend* would never be on your bookshelves right now without the support of publisher Danny Hall, of Vertical Editions.

Thanks so much Danny for having faith in this project and for supporting us through it – and thanks also to photographers Nicola Parker and Richard Markham for your expertise, and to Phil Kelly for your proofreading help.

Finally, my thank to the people of Mansfield and Nottingham in particular and all who have supported me in my long boxing career. I hope you enjoy reading *The Legend* as much as I have working on it.